MATH Trailblazers®

A BALANCED MATHEMATICS PROGRAM INTEGRATING SCIENCE AND LANGUAGE ARTS

Unit Resource Guide
Unit 6
Place Value Patterns

THIRD EDITION

KENDALL/HUNT PUBLISHING COMPANY
4050 Westmark Drive   Dubuque, Iowa 52002

A TIMS® Curriculum
University of Illinois at Chicago

UIC The University of Illinois
at Chicago

The original edition was based on work supported by the National Science Foundation under grant No. MDR 9050226 and the University of Illinois at Chicago. Any opinions, findings, and conclusions or recommendations expressed in this publication are those of the author(s) and do not necessarily reflect the views of the granting agencies.

Letter Home

Place Value Patterns

Date: _____

Dear Family Member:

Have you ever said: *"I've got a million things to do,"* or *"I've told you a million times. . . "*? Through this unit's activities, students will learn what a million really is as they explore patterns in our place value system. Students will complete hands-on activities to help them "see" 1,000,000.

The class will use round numbers to answer questions that do not require an exact answer. Much of the math we do in life requires making good estimates quickly, rather than computing exactly. As with most skills, students need lots of practice to get better with estimation.

You can help your child at home in the following ways:

Numbers such as 4 million are discussed using number lines.

- Ask your child about the *Newswire* in the classroom. Help your child find newspaper articles that include large numbers. Practice reading these numbers with your child. He or she can take these numbers to school to add to the newswire.
- After your child has played the games *Draw, Place, and Read* and *9 to 5 War* at school, encourage him or her to bring the games home so you can play together.
- In this unit, we will focus on the math facts for the nines. Practice the multiplication facts with your child using the *Triangle Flash Cards.*
- Provide opportunities for your child to estimate numbers. If you are traveling, estimate the number of miles you will travel or the amount of time your trip will take.

Sincerely,

_____

Carta al hogar

Patrones de valores posicionales

Fecha: _____

Estimado miembro de familia:

¿Alguna vez ha dicho: *"Tengo un millón de cosas que hacer"* o *"Te lo he dicho un millón de veces. . . "?* Mediante las actividades de esta unidad, los estudiantes aprenderán qué es realmente un millón a medida que exploran patrones en nuestro sistema de valor posicional. Los estudiantes harán actividades prácticas que les ayudarán a "ver" 1,000,000.

Los estudiantes usarán números redondeados para contestar preguntas que no requieren una respuesta exacta. Gran parte de las matemáticas que empleamos en la vida cotidiana requieren hacer buenas estimaciones rápidamente, en lugar de calcular en forma exacta. Como la mayoría de las habilidades, los estudiantes necesitan mucha práctica para hacer mejores estimaciones.

Hablamos de números como 4 millones usando la recta numérica.

Usted puede ayudar a su hijo/a en casa de las siguientes maneras:

- Pregúntele a su hijo/a acerca del "Newswire" de la clase. Ayúdele a buscar artículos en el periódico que contengan números grandes. Practique a leer estos números con su hijo/a. Luego, su hijo/a traerá estos números a la escuela para agregarlos al "newswire".

- Después de que su hijo/a haya jugado a los juegos "Extraer, ubicar y leer" y "Guerra 9 contra 5" en la escuela, pídale que traiga los juegos a casa para que jueguen juntos.

- En esta unidad, pondremos énfasis en la tabla de multiplicación del 9. Practique las tablas de multiplicación con su hijo/a usando las tarjetas triangulares. Mientras trabaja con las tarjetas, pregunte sobre las estrategias para aprender a dividir por nueve.

- Déle a su hijo/a oportunidades de estimar números. Si van de viaje, estimen el número de millas que van a recorrer o el tiempo que durará el viaje.

Atentamente,

_____

Table of Contents

Unit 6
Place Value Patterns

Unit 6

Outline
Place Value Patterns

Unit Summary

Estimated Class Sessions **8-15**

This unit focuses on number sense and numeration. Students explore numbers in the thousands, ten thousands, hundred thousands, and millions. They collect articles from newspapers that have large numbers and place them in order on a newswire. They also work together as a class to build models that extend the base-ten pieces to the millions. Collecting data from the real world extends students' opportunities to develop an intuition about numbers. Students learn to read and write big numbers, which leads to computing with larger numbers. They practice two types of estimation: estimating sums and differences and estimating the number of objects in a collection.

Computational estimation is guided by using convenient numbers, benchmarks, and rounding techniques. When students estimate "how many," they determine if an estimate is close to the actual number by using 10 percent as a guide. In succeeding units, 10% continues as a standard for estimation. In the context of an ancient story about the inventor of the game of chess, students explore the patterns of the powers of two using diagrams, data tables, and graphs. The DPP for this unit reviews the multiplication facts and provides practice with the division facts for the nines.

Major Concept Focus

- Student Rubric: *Knowing*
- place value to the millions
- exponents
- reading and writing large numbers
- convenient numbers
- 10% as a standard for error analysis
- powers of two and ten
- using diagrams to solve problems
- computational estimation
- estimating the number of objects in a collection
- ordering large numbers
- multiplication and division facts for the nines

Pacing Suggestions

The unit includes two optional lessons:

* Lesson 5 *Close Enough* discusses accuracy in estimation and measurement. Students learn to use 10 percent as a benchmark to judge the accuracy of their estimates. This concept is then applied in the *Volume vs. Number* laboratory investigation in Unit 8, as well as in laboratory investigations in future units. If you elect to omit this lesson, you will need to skip related questions in subsequent lessons.

* Lesson 7 *9 to 5 War* provides multiplication math facts practice in a game setting.

Assessment Indicators

Use the following Assessment Indicators and the *Observational Assessment Record* that follows the Background section in this unit to assess students on key ideas.

A1. Can students read and write large numbers (to the millions)?

A2. Can students compare and order large numbers (to the millions)?

A3. Can students represent large numbers (to the millions) using place value charts and number lines?

A4. Can students use patterns to make predictions?

A5. Can students estimate sums and differences for large numbers?

A6. Do students demonstrate fluency with the multiplication facts for the 9s?

A7. Can students write the four number sentences in the fact families for the 9s?

Unit Planner

KEY: SG = Student Guide, DAB = Discovery Assignment Book, AB = Adventure Book, URG = Unit Resource Guide, DPP = Daily Practice and Problems, HP = Home Practice (found in Discovery Assignment Book), and TIG = Teacher Implementation Guide.

	Lesson Information	Supplies	Copies/Transparencies

Lesson 1

Newswire

URG Pages 25–36
SG Pages 150–153
DAB Page 73
DPP A–B
HP Parts 1 & 5

Estimated Class Sessions

1

Activity
Students collect large numbers from newspapers. They arrange the numbers in numerical order on a wire (clothesline) in the classroom.

Math Facts
DPP Bit A begins review and practice of the nines multiplication facts.

Homework
1. Assign the Homework section in the *Student Guide*. Students look for numbers in newspapers at home. They bring in the numbers and add them to the newswire.
2. Assign Parts 1 and 5 of the Home Practice.

Assessment
Use the *Observational Assessment Record* to note students' abilities to read and order large numbers.

Supplies:
- newspapers
- highlighter markers, optional
- string, twine, or cord for the newswire
- 4 paper clips or clothespins per student pair
- 1 pair of scissors per student pair
- paper hole punch
- 2 3-by-5-inch index cards cut in half lengthwise per student pair
- envelopes for storing flash cards

Copies/Transparencies:
- 1 transparency of *Place Value Chart* DAB Page 73
- 1 copy of *Observational Assessment Record* URG Pages 11–12 to be used throughout this unit

Lesson 2

Doubles

URG Pages 37–51
SG Pages 154–156
DPP C–F
HP Part 2

Estimated Class Sessions

2-3

Activity
Students read a story about the inventor of the game of chess who asks for a specific reward. Within this context, students investigate doubling patterns and develop number sense for large numbers.

Math Facts
DPP Bit C provides practice with the multiplication facts for the nines.

Homework
1. Assign the Homework section of the *Doubles* Activity Pages.
2. Assign Home Practice Part 2.

Assessment
1. Use DPP item D as an assessment.
2. Score homework *Question 1* using the Telling dimension of the *TIMS Multidimensional Rubric*.

Supplies:
- several colored pencils
- 2 large sheets of paper, optional

Copies/Transparencies:
- 1 copy of *Three-column Data Table* URG Page 47 per student, optional
- 1 copy of *Centimeter Graph Paper* URG Page 48 per student
- 1 transparency of *Three-column Data Table* URG Page 47, optional
- 1 copy of *TIMS Multidimensional Rubric* TIG, Assessment section
- 50 copies of *10,000 Sq Mm Grid* URG Page 49, optional

Lesson 3

Big Base-Ten Pieces

URG Pages 52–65
SG Pages 157–159
DAB Page 75
DPP G–J
HP Part 3

Estimated Class Sessions

2-3

Activity
Students are introduced to the powers of 10 using a place value chart. They also build large base-ten pieces to represent ten thousand, one hundred thousand, and one million.

Math Facts
DPP items G, H, and J provide practice with math facts.

Homework
1. Students play the game *Draw, Place, and Read* at home.
2. Assign Home Practice Part 3.

Assessment
Use the Journal Prompt as an assessment.

Supplies:
- 1 meterstick per student group and 24 for the teacher
- masking tape
- 6–16 base-ten packs
- 4–8 rulers
- paper for covering the big base-ten pieces, optional

Copies/Transparencies:
- 1 copy of *Digit Cards 0–9* URG Pages 61–62 per student group copied back to back
- 1 transparency of *Place Value Chart II* URG Page 63

	Lesson Information	**Supplies**	**Copies/ Transparencies**

Lesson 4

News Number Line

URG Pages 66–76
SG Pages 160–163
DPP K–L
HP Part 6

Estimated Class Sessions
1

Activity
The class newswire is converted into a number line. Large numbers collected from newspapers are placed in order on this number line.

Math Facts
DPP items K and L provide practice with multiplication and division facts.

Homework
1. Assign the homework in the *Student Guide.* Omit *Questions 8–10* if Lesson 5 will be omitted.
2. Assign Part 6 of the Home Practice.

Assessment
1. Use homework *Questions 5–7* as a quiz.
2. Use the *Observational Assessment Record* to note students' abilities to order large numbers.

• number newswire created in Lesson 1
• 1 or 10 metersticks
• red and green markers
• 10-meter strip of adding machine tape, string, twine, or cord
• 1 calculator per student group
• paper clips

Lesson 5

Close Enough

URG Pages 77–90
SG Pages 164–168
DAB Page 77

Estimated Class Sessions
2-3

OPTIONAL LESSON
Optional Activity
Students use 10 percent as a benchmark to establish whether or not an estimate is close to an actual amount.

Homework
Assign the Homework section in the *Student Guide.*

Assessment
Use *Questions 1–2* in the Homework section as an assessment.

• 1 calculator per student
• meterstick
• clear centimeter ruler
• mystery jar from Lesson 4 homework
• clear jar filled with 123 objects, optional
• large and small clear jars, optional
• objects for estimation such as connecting cubes, marbles, or beans, optional

• 1 copy of *Three-column Data Table* URG Page 47 per student group, optional
• 1 transparency of *10% Chart* DAB Page 77 or large paper for class data table
• 1 transparency of *Three-column Data Table* URG Page 47, optional

---

Lesson 6

Using Estimation

URG Pages 91–109
SG Pages 169–174
DPP M–P
HP Parts 4 & 7

Estimated Class Sessions
2-3

Activity
Students use a number line to find convenient numbers expressed to the nearest 1000, 10,000, 100,000, and 1,000,000. They practice paper-and-pencil procedures for addition and subtraction.

Math Facts
DPP item M provides practice with math facts for the nines. Bit O is a short quiz on the multiplication facts for the nines.

Homework
1. Assign *Questions 1–4* in the Homework section after Part 1.
2. Assign *Questions 5–12* in the Homework section after Part 2.
3. Assign Parts 4 and 7 of the Home Practice.

• 1 copy of *Check-Up Time* URG Pages 102–103 per student
• 1 copy of *Individual Assessment Record Sheet* TIG Assessment section per student, previously copied for use throughout the year
• 1 copy of *TIMS Multidimensional Rubric* TIG, Assessment section
• 1 transparency or poster of Student Rubric: *Knowing* TIG, Assessment section
• 1 transparency of a blank number line, optional

(Continued)

	Lesson Information	Supplies	Copies/Transparencies

Assessment
1. Students complete the skill assessment *Check-Up Time.*
2. Use DPP item O *Multiplication Quiz: 9s* as an assessment.
3. Use the Knowing dimension of the *TIMS Multidimensional Rubric* to assess students' abilities to use computational estimation.
4. Use the *Observational Assessment Record* to document students' abilities to represent larger numbers on number lines and estimate sums and differences.
5. Transfer appropriate documentation from the Unit 6 *Observational Assessment Record* to students' *Individual Assessment Record Sheets.*

Lesson 7

9 to 5 War

URG Pages 110–115
SG Pages 175–177
DAB Pages 79–82

Estimated Class Sessions

1

OPTIONAL LESSON

Optional Game
Students draw cards from decks to find products of multiplication facts for the fives and nines.

Math Facts
The *9 to 5 War* Game provides practice with multiplication facts for the fives and nines.

Homework
Ask students to play the game at home.

• 1 pair of scissors per student pair
• 1 calculator per student pair
• 1 deck of playing cards with face cards removed per student pair, optional

• 2 copies of *Digit Cards 0–9* URG Pages 61–62 per student copied back to back
• 1 table from *Small Multiplication Tables* URG Page 115 per student

---

Preparing for Upcoming Lessons

In an optional lesson, Lesson 5, students will estimate the number of objects in jars. If students are to complete this lesson, assign them the task of preparing a mystery jar by filling (or partially filling) a clear jar with the same kind of object. See the Homework section in Lesson 4 and Before the Activity in Lesson 5 for details.

Connections

A current list of literature and software connections is available at *www.mathtrailblazers.com.* You can also find information on connections in the *Teacher Implementation Guide* Literature List and Software List sections.

Literature Connections

Suggested Titles

- Birch, David. *The King's Chessboard.* Penguin Putnam Books, New York, 1993. (Lesson 2)
- Demi. *One Grain of Rice.* Scholastic Press, Inc., New York, 1997.
- Handford, Martin. *Where's Waldo?* Candlewick Press, Cambridge, MA, 1997. (Lesson 5)
- McKissack, Patricia. *A Million Fish . . . More or Less.* Random House, New York, 1996. (Lesson 6)
- Pittman, Helena Clare. *A Grain of Rice.* Bantam Doubleday Dell, New York, 1996. (Lesson 2)
- Schwartz, David. *How Much Is a Million?* William Morrow and Company, New York, 1993. (Lesson 6)

Software Connections

- *Carmen Sandiego's Math Detective* provides practice with math facts, estimation, ordering numbers, and word problems.
- *Math Arena* is a collection of math activities that reinforces many math concepts.
- *Math Munchers Deluxe* provides practice in basic facts and finding equivalent fractions, decimals, and percents in an arcade-like game.
- *Mighty Math Calculating Crew* poses short answer questions about number operations and money skills.
- *Mighty Math Number Heroes* poses short answer questions about number operations.
- *National Library of Virtual Manipulatives* website (http:matti.usu.edu) allows students to work with manipulatives including base-ten pieces, the abacus, and many others.

Teaching All Math Trailblazers Students

Math Trailblazers® lessons are designed for students with a wide range of abilities. The lessons are flexible and do not require significant adaptation for diverse learning styles or academic levels. However, when needed, lessons can be tailored to allow students to engage their abilities to the greatest extent possible while building knowledge and skills.

To assist you in meeting the needs of all students in your classroom, this section contains information about some of the features in the curriculum that allow all students access to mathematics. For additional information, see the Teaching the *Math Trailblazers* Student: Meeting Individual Needs section in the *Teacher Implementation Guide*.

Differentiation Opportunities in this Unit

Games

Use games to promote or extend understanding of math concepts and to practice skills with children who need more practice.

- *Draw, Place, and Read* from Lesson 3 *Big Base-Ten Pieces*
- Lesson 7 *9 to 5 War*

Journal Prompts

Journal prompts provide opportunities for students to explain and reflect on mathematical problems. They can help both students who need practice explaining their ideas and students who benefit from answering higher order questions. Students with various learning styles can express themselves using pictures, words, and sentences. Teachers can alter journal prompts to suit students' ability levels. The following lessons contain a journal prompt:

- Lesson 2 *Doubles*
- Lesson 3 *Big Base-Ten Pieces*
- Lesson 4 *News Number Line*
- Lesson 5 *Close Enough*
- Lesson 6 *Using Estimation*
- Lesson 7 *9 to 5 War*

DPP Challenges

DPP Challenges are items from the Daily Practice and Problems that usually take more than fifteen minutes to complete. These problems are more thought-provoking and can be used to stretch students' problem-solving skills. The following lessons have a DPP Challenge in them:

- DPP Challenge L from Lesson 4 *News Number Line*
- DPP Challenge N from Lesson 6 *Using Estimation*

Extensions

Use extensions to enrich lessons. Many extensions provide opportunities to further involve or challenge students of all abilities. Take a moment to review the extensions prior to beginning this unit. Some extensions may require additional preparation and planning. The following lessons contain extensions:

- Lesson 2 *Doubles*
- Lesson 5 *Close Enough*
- Lesson 6 *Using Estimation*

Unit 6

Background
Place Value Patterns

A child's understanding of numbers occurs gradually. Children need many opportunities to work with numbers in real world contexts to develop an intuition about numbers—what is called number sense. They also need an understanding of place value for later work with computation.

Place Value and Number Sense

This unit provides many opportunities for students to explore number meaning and to develop number sense. Students collect large numbers from newspapers and magazines. They then explore place value as they practice reading and ordering these numbers. They extend the base-ten pieces for 1, 10, 100, and 1000 by building physical models of 10,000, 100,000, and 1,000,000. This provides an opportunity for students to see the relative size of numbers as they explore the patterns in our place value system. Students gain experience using numbers written as symbols as they link the numbers to names and physical models.

Estimation and Number Sense

Estimation is a tool that leads to better number sense. Students explore strategies for computational estimation in this unit. Students who are able to estimate well tend to be more flexible in their thinking, use a variety of estimation strategies, and demonstrate a deeper understanding of numbers and operations.

While there are times when exact answers are necessary in computing large numbers, an estimate is often all that is needed or possible. Rounding numbers is introduced as one strategy for computational estimation. Using round numbers allows us to compute mentally. This unit's emphasis is not on the rules for rounding numbers but on the context in which round numbers are used. Reliance on a rule may lead to confusion and unreasonable

solutions. Students need to pay attention to the value of the numbers in each context. One reason we use round numbers is to estimate approximate answers to addition, subtraction, multiplication, and division problems so we can compute easier in our heads.

In an optional lesson, Lesson 5 *Close Enough,* students practice estimating the number of objects in a collection by estimating the number of objects in a mystery jar. They then find the actual number of objects in their jar to see if their estimates are close. The class determines a standard for deciding if an estimate is "close enough."

Students need to discuss when estimation is appropriate and when exact answers are needed. This unit provides activities in which this discussion can occur. See the TIMS Tutors: *Estimation, Accuracy, and Error* and *Arithmetic* in the *Teacher Implementation Guide* for more information on estimation strategies.

Resources

- Gamow, George. *One Two Three . . . Infinity: Facts and Speculations of Science.* Dover Publications, Mineola, NY, 1988.
- Hopkins, Lindy, and Jean Shaw (eds.). "Popping Up Number Sense," in *Teaching Children Mathematics,* October 1995.
- Hyde, Arthur, and Pamela Hyde. *Mathwise, Teaching Mathematical Thinking and Problem Solving.* Heinemann, Portsmouth, NH, 1991.
- Joslyn, Ruth. "Using Concrete Models to Teach Large-Number Concepts," in *The Arithmetic Teacher.* November 1990, pp. 6–9.
- Kasner, Edward, and James Newman. "Pastimes of Past and Present Times," in *The World of Mathematics.* Notes by James Newman. Simon and Schuster, New York, 1960.

- National Research Council. "Developing Proficiency with Whole Numbers," in *Adding It Up: Helping Children Learn Mathematics.* J. Kilpatrick, J. Swafford, and B. Findell, eds. National Academy Press, Washington, DC, 2001.
- Phillips, Elizabeth, et al. *Patterns and Functions* from the Curriculum and Evaluation Standards Addenda Series, Grades 5–8. National Council of Teachers of Mathematics, Reston, VA, 1992.
- *Principles and Standards for School Mathematics.* National Council of Teachers of Mathematics, Reston, VA, 2000.
- Sowder, Judith. "Estimation and Number Sense," in *Handbook of Research on Mathematics Teaching and Learning.* D.A. Grouws (ed.). Macmillan Publishing Company, New York, 1992, pp. 371–389.
- *The World Almanac for Kids 2003.* Kevin Seabrooke (ed.). World Almanac Education Group, Inc., New York, 2002.

Observational Assessment Record

(A1) Can students read and write large numbers (to the millions)?

(A2) Can students compare and order large numbers (to the millions)?

(A3) Can students represent large numbers (to the millions) using place value charts and number lines?

(A4) Can students use patterns to make predictions?

(A5) Can students estimate sums and differences for large numbers?

(A6) Do students demonstrate fluency with the multiplication facts for the 9s?

(A7) Can students write the four number sentences in the fact families for the 9s?

(A8) _____

Name	A1	A2	A3	A4	A5	A6	A7	A8	Comments
1.									
2.									
3.									
4.									
5.									
6.									
7.									
8.									
9.									
10.									
11.									
12.									
13.									

Name	A1	A2	A3	A4	A5	A6	A7	A8	Comments
14.									
15.									
16.									
17.									
18.									
19.									
20.									
21.									
22.									
23.									
24.									
25.									
26.									
27.									
28.									
29.									
30.									
31.									
32.									

Unit 6

Daily Practice and Problems
Place Value Patterns

A DPP Menu for Unit 6

Two Daily Practice and Problems (DPP) items are included for each class session listed in the Unit Outline. A scope and sequence chart for the DPP is in the *Teacher Implementation Guide*.

Icons in the Teacher Notes column designate the subject matter of each DPP item. The first item in each class session is always a Bit and the second is either a Task or Challenge. Each item falls into one or more of the categories listed below. A menu of the DPP items for Unit 6 follows.

N Number Sense	✖ Computation	⏱ Time	◳ Geometry
B, D–F, H, I, L, N, P	B, E, F, I, N,	H	
⁵⁄₇ Math Facts	$ Money	⚖ Measurement	▨ Data
A, C, G, H, J–M, O	I	P	E

Practice and Assessment of the Multiplication Facts

By the end of fourth grade, students in *Math Trailblazers* are expected to demonstrate fluency with all the multiplication and division facts. The DPP for this unit continues the systematic strategies-based approach to reviewing the multiplication facts and learning the division facts. This unit focuses on the fourth group of facts, the nines.

The *Triangle Flash Cards* for the nines follows the Home Practice for this unit in the *Discovery Assignment Book*. A discussion of the flash cards is in item A of the DPP.

A quiz on the nines is provided in item O. Items C, G, H, J, K, and M provide practice with the multiplication and division facts for the nines.

For more information about the distribution and assessment of the math facts, see the TIMS Tutor: *Math Facts* in the *Teacher Implementation Guide*. Also refer to the DPP guide in the *Unit Resource Guide* for Unit 3.

Students may solve the items individually, in groups, or as a class. The items may also be assigned for homework. The DPPs are also available on the Teacher Resource CD.

Student Questions	Teacher Notes

 Triangle Flash Cards: 9s

With a partner, use your *Triangle Flash Cards* to quiz each other on the multiplication facts for the nines. One partner covers the shaded corner displaying the highest number. This number will be the answer to a multiplication fact, called the product. The second person multiplies the other two numbers. These two are the factors.

Separate the used cards into three piles: those facts you know and can answer quickly, those you can figure out with a strategy, and those you need to learn. Practice the last two piles again and then list the facts you need to practice at home for homework.

Circle the facts you know quickly on your *Multiplication Facts I Know* chart.

TIMS Bit

The *Triangle Flash Cards* follow the Home Practice in the *Discovery Assignment Book*. Part 1 of the Home Practice reminds students to bring home for homework the list of facts they need to practice. Also send home the *Triangle Flash Cards*.

Have students circle the facts they know well on their *Multiplication Facts I Know* charts. Remind students that if they know a fact, they also know its turn-around fact. Since these charts can also be used as multiplication tables, students should have them available to use as needed.

Inform students when you will give the quiz on the 9s. This quiz appears in TIMS Bit O.

Arithmetic Review

Do these problems with paper and pencil or mental math, not with calculators.

1. A. $\begin{array}{r} 239 \\ -\ 65 \\ \hline \end{array}$ B. $\begin{array}{r} 468 \\ +113 \\ \hline \end{array}$

   C. $\begin{array}{r} 906 \\ -\ 18 \\ \hline \end{array}$ D. $\begin{array}{r} 750 \\ -250 \\ \hline \end{array}$

   E. $46 + 106 + 31 =$

   F. $1005 + 9 + 240 =$

2. Arrange your answers from smallest to largest.

3. Which answer is closest to 700?

4. Explain how you solved Question 1C.

TIMS Task

1. A. 174   B. 581
   C. 888   D. 500
   E. 183   F. 1254

2. 174, 183, 500, 581, 888, 1254

3. 581

4. Possible strategy: First
   subtract 6 from 906:
   906 − 6 = 900.
   Then subtract 12 more
   in two steps: 900 − 10 = 890
   and 890 − 2 = 888.

Patterns

Complete:

$1 \times 9 =$

$2 \times 9 =$

$3 \times 9 =$

$4 \times 9 =$

$5 \times 9 =$

$6 \times 9 =$

$7 \times 9 =$

$8 \times 9 =$

$9 \times 9 =$

$10 \times 9 =$

What patterns do you see?

TIMS Bit

Observing patterns helps students remember the facts for the nines. Patterns include:

1. When products are listed in a column, the digits in the tens' place count up by ones $(0, 1, 2, 3, \ldots)$ and the digits in the ones' place count down by ones $(9, 8, 7, \ldots)$.

2. The sum of the digits in each product is nine. For example, 36 is the product of 4×9. The sum of 3 and 6 is nine. This provides a strategy for checking multiplication by nine: Does $9 \times 6 = 54$ or 56? It must be 54 since $5 + 4 = 9$, but $5 + 6$ is not 9.

3. You can easily derive the nines from the tens. For example, 10×4 is 40. So, 9×4 is 4 less: $40 - 4 = 36$.

Student Questions	Teacher Notes

 The Long and the Short

TIMS Task

Write the following numbers in words:

A. 421   B. 8536

C. 58,972   D. 20,380

Write the following words as numbers:

E. six thousand nineteen

F. two thousand, three hundred forty-one

G. two hundred one thousand,
five hundred two

A. four hundred twenty-one

B. eight thousand, five hundred thirty-six

C. fifty-eight thousand, nine hundred seventy-two

D. twenty thousand, three hundred eighty

E. 6019

F. 2341

G. 201,502

 Median and Mean

TIMS Bit

1. Median: 52 cm

2. Mean: 51 cm

Ming experimented with 3 kinds of balls to find out which one bounced highest. He dropped each type of ball five times from 1 meter.

Here are the bounce heights for the tennis ball: 52 cm, 47 cm, 55 cm, 52 cm, and 50 cm.

1. Find the median bounce height.

2. Use a calculator to find the mean bounce height to the nearest cm.

The Mystery Unfolds

TIMS Task

1. Fold a sheet of paper in half. Now unfold it. How many sections are there?

2. Fold the paper in half again. This time without unfolding, fold it in half once more. Now unfold it. How many sections are there?

3. Complete the following data table by folding your paper in half 3, 4, and 5 times:

Number of Folds	Number of Sections	Number of Sections Written with Exponents
1	2	2^1
2		2^2
3		

4. What patterns do you see?

5. Predict the number of sections after the paper has been folded in half 6 times.

Teacher Notes

1. 2

2. 4

3.

Number of Folds	Number of Sections	Number of Sections Written with Exponents
1	2	2^1
2	4	2^2
3	8	2^3
4	16	2^4
5	32	2^5

4. Answers will vary. Students may notice that the number in the second column keeps doubling and that the exponent in the third column is equal to the number of folds.

5. $2^6 = 64$

| Student Questions | Teacher Notes |

 Nines Are Fine

Do these problems in your head. Write only the answers. Write a division number sentence in the same fact family for each one.

A. $9 \times 5 =$

B. $9 \times 7 =$

C. $8 \times 9 =$

D. $9 \times 2 =$

E. $6 \times 9 =$

F. $9 \times 4 =$

G. $10 \times 9 =$

H. $9 \times 9 =$

I. $9 \times 3 =$

J. $1 \times 9 =$

TIMS Bit

Ask students what strategies they use to solve these problems. One possible strategy for finding nine times a number is to multiply the number by ten, then subtract the number from the total. (Example: $9 \times 6 = 10 \times 6 - 6$.) See Bit C for more strategies.

A. 45	B. 63
C. 72	D. 18
E. 54	F. 36
G. 90	H. 81
I. 27	J. 9

Answers will vary for the division sentences.

H **Calculator Counting**

1. Use a calculator to count by 3s to 100. Work with a partner. One partner will count, saying the numbers quietly. The other partner will time how long the counting takes. Take turns. How long did it take? Can you land on 100?

2. Use the data from Question 1 to predict how long it would take to count by 9s to 100. Then, use a calculator to count by 9s to 100. How long did it take? Can you land on 100?

TIMS Task

Students may work in pairs for this activity. To skip count by 3s on a calculator with a constant function, students press:

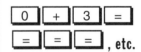, etc.

Did students count three times as fast by 9s as by 3s? Since 100 is not a multiple of 3 or 9, you cannot land on 100 when skip counting by 3 or 9.

Ana's Purchase

1. Ana bought a gallon of milk for $2.49, a box of crackers for $1.56, and a magazine for $2.95. Will $10.00 be enough to pay the bill?

2. About how much change will Ana get back?

TIMS Bit

1. Yes. Students can use convenient numbers to quickly determine this answer in their head.

2. Her purchases cost about $2.50 + $1.50 + $3.00 = $7.00. She'll get back about $3.00.

 Mr. and Mrs. Head

Mr. Head says that $9 \times 5 = 46$, and Mrs. Head cannot convince him he's wrong. Write a letter to Mr. Head explaining what 9×5 equals and why. You may use drawings in your letter.

TIMS Task

Possible solutions include skip counting, drawing pictures of 9 groups of 5 things, drawing a 9×5 array, and reasoning that since 10×5 is 50 and 9×5 is 5 less, 9×5 must be 45. Or, since the sum of the digits of 46 is not 9 ($4 + 6 \neq 9$), then 9×5 cannot equal 46. Also, all multiples of 5 end in 5 or 0; thus 46 is not a possible product.

Fact Families for × and ÷

Complete the number sentences for the related facts.

A. $3 \times 9 =$ ____

　　____ $\div 3 =$ ____

　　____ $\div 9 =$ ____

　　____ $\times 3 =$ ____

B. $9 \times 7 =$ ____

　　____ $\div 7 =$ ____

　　____ $\div 9 =$ ____

　　$7 \times$ ____ $=$ ____

C. $9 \times 9 =$ ____

　　____ $\div 9 =$ ____

D. $54 \div 9 =$ ____

　　$9 \times$ ____ $= 54$

　　$54 \div$ ____ $= 9$

　　____ $\times 9 =$ ____

E. $9 \times 4 =$ ____

　　____ $\div 9 = 4$

　　____ $\div 4 =$ ____

　　____ $\times 9 =$ ____

TIMS Bit　

A. 27; 27 ÷ 3 = 9;
　　27 ÷ 9 = 3;
　　9 × 3 = 27

B. 63; 63 ÷ 7 = 9;
　　63 ÷ 9 = 7;
　　7 × 9 = 63

C. 81; 81 ÷ 9 = 9

D. 6; 9 × 6 = 54;
　　54 ÷ 6 = 9;
　　6 × 9 = 54

E. 36; 36 ÷ 9 = 4;
　　36 ÷ 4 = 9;
　　4 × 9 = 36

Who Am I?

1. I am a square number greater than 9. One of my two digits is 5 more than the other. Who am I?

2. I am a square number less than 100. One of my digits is 8 less than twice the other. Who am I?

3. Make up your own square number riddle and try it on a partner.

TIMS Challenge

Answers will vary.

1. 16 or 49

2. 25 or 64

3. Answers will vary. Have some students present their riddles to the whole class.

 More Fine Nines

Do these problems in your head. Write the answers and then write the other number sentences in the same fact family.

A. $9 \times 3 =$

B. $9 \times 2 =$

C. $63 \div 9 =$

D. $8 \times 9 =$

E. $81 \div 9 =$

F. $9 \times 4 =$

G. $10 \times 9 =$

H. $54 \div 9 =$

I. $5 \times 9 =$

TIMS Bit

Ask students what strategies they use to solve these problems.

A. 27; $3 \times 9 = 27$; $27 \div 9 = 3$; $27 \div 3 = 9$

B. 18; $2 \times 9 = 18$; $18 \div 9 = 2$; $18 \div 2 = 9$

C. 7; $63 \div 7 = 9$; $7 \times 9 = 63$; $9 \times 7 = 63$

D. 72; $9 \times 8 = 72$; $72 \div 9 = 8$; $72 \div 8 = 9$

E. 9; $9 \times 9 = 81$

F. 36; $4 \times 9 = 36$; $36 \div 4 = 9$; $36 \div 9 = 4$

G. 90; $9 \times 10 = 90$; $90 \div 9 = 10$; $90 \div 10 = 9$

H. 6; $54 \div 6 = 9$; $6 \times 9 = 54$; $9 \times 6 = 54$

I. 45; $9 \times 5 = 45$; $45 \div 9 = 5$; $45 \div 5 = 9$

Flying Rumors

I.M. Polite told a rumor to two people on the first day of school. On the second day, the two people who heard the rumor each told the rumor to two more people. On the third day, the four people who heard the rumor on the second day each told it to two more people.

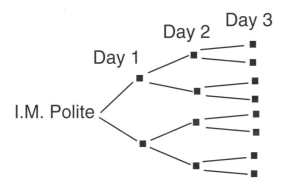

1. If this pattern is continued, how many new people will hear the rumor for the first time on the tenth day? How did you decide?

2. How many total people will know the rumor on the sixth day? How did you decide?

3. There are 500 people in the school. On what day will the whole school know the rumor? Show how you did this problem.

TIMS Challenge

1. 1024

2. 127

3. On the 8th day. Solution strategies will vary. One way is to organize the information into a chart. Students may write the number of new people as a power of two (using exponents).

Day of School	New People	Total People
1	$2 \times 1 =$ $2^1 = 2$	3
2	$2 \times 2 =$ $2^2 = 4$	7
3	$2 \times 2 \times 2 =$ $2^3 = 8$	15
4	$2^4 = 16$	31
5	$2^5 = 32$	63
6	$2^6 = 64$	127
7	$2^7 = 128$	255
8	$2^8 = 256$	511

Discussion question: How can you figure out the total number of people that know the rumor if you know the number of the day (n)? Possible answer: Fill in the table by doubling the number of new people. To find the total number of people, double the number of new people and subtract 1.

Student Questions	Teacher Notes

 Multiplication Quiz: 9s

A. $3 \times 9 =$ B. $9 \times 7 =$

C. $10 \times 9 =$ D. $2 \times 9 =$

E. $5 \times 9 =$ F. $9 \times 8 =$

G. $6 \times 9 =$ H. $4 \times 9 =$

I. $9 \times 9 =$ J. $9 \times 1 =$

TIMS Bit

This quiz is on the fourth group of multiplication facts, the nines. We recommend 2 minutes for this quiz. Allow students to change pens or pencils after the time is up and complete the remaining problems in a different color.

After students take the test, have them update their *Multiplication Facts I Know* charts.

P **Which Is Closest?**

1. Which number is closest to 4056?

   450   4000   4100   5000

2. Which number is closest to 62,096?

   7000   60,000   65,000   70,000

3. Which is a reasonable estimate for the height of a 5-story apartment building?

   30 feet   50 feet   300 feet   500 feet

TIMS Task

1. 4100
2. 60,000
3. 50 feet; strategies may include estimating the height of the classroom (about 10 feet), then multiplying by 5 stories.

Lesson 1

Newswire

Lesson Overview

Students begin work on an activity in which they read, write, and order large numbers. In this lesson, students find large numbers in newspapers and order them on a newswire stretched across the classroom. In Lesson 4, students will convert the newswire to a number line and space the numbers appropriately to show the magnitude of each number.

Key Content

- Reading and writing large numbers (to the millions).
- Comparing and ordering large numbers (to the millions).
- Connecting mathematics and science to real-world situations.
- Developing number sense for large numbers (to the millions).
- Understanding place value (to the millions).

Key Vocabulary

- acre
- millions
- ones
- period
- place value
- thousands

Math Facts

DPP Bit A begins review and practice of the nines multiplication facts.

Homework

1. Assign the Homework section in the *Student Guide*. Students look for numbers in newspapers at home. They bring in the numbers and add them to the newswire.
2. Assign Parts 1 and 5 of the Home Practice.

Assessment

Use the *Observational Assessment Record* to note students' abilities to read and order large numbers.

Curriculum Sequence

Before This Unit

Large Numbers

Students learned to read and write numbers in the thousands in Grade 3 Unit 4.

After This Unit

Large Numbers

Students will revisit large numbers in Grade 5 Unit 2. They will further develop their abilities to estimate and compute with large numbers.

Materials List

Supplies and Copies

Student	Teacher
Supplies for Each Student Pair • newspaper • highlighter markers, optional • 4 paper clips or clothespins • scissors • 2 3-by-5-inch index cards cut in half lengthwise • envelopes for storing flash cards	**Supplies** • paper hole punch • string, twine, or cord for the newswire
Copies	**Copies/Transparencies** • 1 transparency of *Place Value Chart* (*Discovery Assignment Book* Page 73) • 1 copy of *Observational Assessment Record* to be used throughout this unit (*Unit Resource Guide* Pages 11–12)

All blackline masters including assessment, transparency, and DPP masters are also on the Teacher Resource CD.

Student Books

Newswire (*Student Guide* Pages 150–153)
Triangle Flash Cards: 9s (*Discovery Assignment Book* Page 71)
Place Value Chart (*Discovery Assignment Book* Page 73)

Daily Practice and Problems and Home Practice

DPP items A–B (*Unit Resource Guide* Pages 14–15)
Home Practice Parts 1 & 5 (*Discovery Assignment Book* Pages 67 & 69)

Note: Classrooms whose pacing differs significantly from the suggested pacing of the units should use the
Math Facts Calendar in Section 4 of the *Facts Resource Guide* to ensure students receive the complete math
facts program.

Assessment Tools

Observational Assessment Record (*Unit Resource Guide* Pages 11–12)

Daily Practice and Problems

Suggestions for using the DPPs are on page 32.

A. Bit: Triangle Flash Cards: 9s [5×7]

(URG p. 14)

With a partner, use your *Triangle Flash Cards* to quiz each other on the multiplication facts for the nines. One partner covers the shaded corner displaying the highest number. This number will be the answer to a multiplication fact, called the product. The second person multiplies the other two numbers. These two are the factors.

Separate the used cards into three piles: those facts you know and can answer quickly, those you can figure out with a strategy, and those you need to learn. Practice the last two piles again and then list the facts you need to practice at home for homework.

Circle the facts you know quickly on your *Multiplication Facts I Know* chart.

B. Task: Arithmetic Review

(URG p. 15)

Do these problems with paper and pencil or mental math, not with calculators.

1. A. $\begin{array}{r} 239 \\ -\ 65 \end{array}$ B. $\begin{array}{r} 468 \\ +\ 113 \end{array}$

    C. $\begin{array}{r} 906 \\ -\ 18 \end{array}$ D. $\begin{array}{r} 750 \\ -\ 250 \end{array}$

    E. $46 + 106 + 31 =$
    F. $1005 + 9 + 240 =$

2. Arrange your answers from smallest to largest.
3. Which answer is closest to 700?
4. Explain how you solved Question 1C.

Before the Activity

Collect enough newspapers to give each pair of students their own paper. Hang the newswire (string, twine, or cord works nicely) in a spot easily accessible to students. They will work with it over the next several days. If possible, hang the wire against a wall to protect the index cards from being knocked off.

It is useful to have a wire at least 5 meters long so several students can work on the wire at one time. Using a 10-meter wire will allow the needed length to convert the wire to a number line in Lesson 4. In Lesson 4, students place the index cards at measured intervals on a number line to illustrate the relative distances between zero, one thousand, one hundred thousand, and one million. Figure 1 shows an example of a number newswire. Figure 2 shows how the newswire will be converted to a number line in Lesson 4.

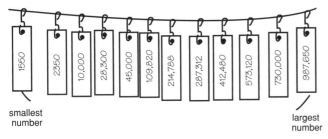

Figure 1: *Newswire*

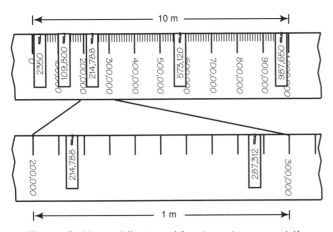

Figure 2: *Use adding machine tape to convert the newswire to a number line.*

Clear space on a bulletin board or wall for students to sort and place their news articles. See Figure 3. Provide space for different size numbers as shown.

TIMS Tip

Rather than hanging the news articles directly on the wire, cut 3-by-5-inch index cards in half lengthwise and punch a hole in the narrow end of each card. Have students copy the numbers they found onto the index card strips. Use an unfolded paper clip to hang the index card strips on the newswire. Pinch both loops of the paper clip so tags are not knocked off the line. See Figure 1. Attaching the index card strips to the wire with clothespins is another option.

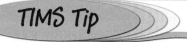

TIMS Tip

Give students a 10-minute time limit to find their numbers, record them on the *Place Value Chart,* and write them on index card strips. You may wish to have extra newspaper clippings available and index cards prepared with numbers between 1000 and 1,000,000. Later, you can add these to the newswire.

TIMS Tip

You will need students' newspaper articles with big numbers again in Lesson 6 *Using Estimation.*

Figure 3: *Newswire bulletin board idea*

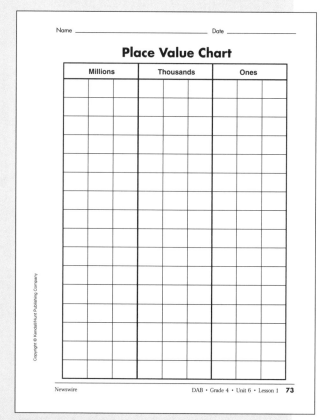

Discovery Assignment Book - page 73

Part 1 Constructing the Newswire

Begin by passing out newspapers and scissors. Ask student pairs to find numbers larger than 1000 in newspaper articles and select one to underline or highlight. Students should cut out the whole paragraph so that there is some context or unit attached to the number. Have student pairs find at least four large numbers written in symbols, not in words. For example, students should choose 1,236,000 and not 1.2 million.

Have students write each number they found on the *Place Value Chart* in their *Discovery Assignment Book.* Students should then carefully write each of their numbers on half an index card so the numbers can be placed on the newswire during this lesson and on the news number line in Lesson 4. See Figure 1.

After students record their numbers on index card strips, have them post the newspaper clippings on the "Newswire Bulletin Board," which has been divided into four sections labeled: "Thousands," "Ten Thousands," "Hundred Thousands," and "A Million or More." See Figure 3. These categories encourage students to think about the relative size of each number. Ask students how they decided in which category to place their articles. Help students discover that they can quickly confirm placement by counting the digits in the number.

Begin a class discussion using prompts such as:

- *Look at the numbers you and your partner found. Which number is the smallest?*

- *Who thinks they have found the smallest number?* (Ask the students who think they have the smallest number to record their number on the *Place Value Chart* transparency.)

- *How can we tell which number is the smallest using the chart?*

- *Can you say each of the numbers listed on the chart in words? How does the chart help us read large numbers?*

Use the *Place Value Chart* transparency during this class discussion to help identify the largest and smallest numbers found. This allows you to model how to record numbers in the chart correctly and allows students to practice reading and ordering numbers.

Demonstrate how to read and write large numbers. Have students isolate each period as they read; say the number formed by the digits within that period; and add the label for that period at the end of the number. For example, the number in Figure 4 is read: thirty-two **million,** seven hundred fifty **thousand,** three hundred sixty-five. For each period, except the **ones'** period, the name of the period is added.

Millions' Period			Thousands' Period			Ones' Period		
	3	2	7	5	0	3	6	5

Figure 4: Place Value Chart *showing the placement of a number*

Once students identify the smallest number, hang the index card strip for that number on the far left side of the newswire. Refer back to the other numbers recorded on the transparency. Ask students to place these numbers in order on the wire to the right of the smallest number. Involve the class in directing students as they read the numbers out loud and place the index card strips on the newswire. Larger numbers are placed to the right and smaller numbers are placed to the left. Repeat the same discussion and procedure asking for the largest number found.

Allow students to choose some of their remaining numbers, read them out loud, and add them to the newswire as time permits. Numbers added to the newswire will need to be inserted between existing numbers, thus providing yet another opportunity for students to think about number relationships. Additional numbers that are brought in as homework can be added to the newswire or saved to use on the number line to be constructed in Lesson 4.

Part 2 **Investigating and Using Patterns in the *Place Value Chart***

Together read the Discuss section of the *Newswire* Activity Pages in the *Student Guide*. Discuss the division of the place value chart into **periods.** Use prompts such as:

* *Describe the pattern in the* Place Value Chart. (Ones, tens, and hundreds repeat in each period.)

* *How does the pattern within each period help make reading and writing numbers easier?* (Students might say that knowing this pattern— ones, tens, hundreds—helps them to say the number within each period. Or, it is just like reading smaller numbers and then adding the name of the period to what you say.)

* *We usually divide periods with a comma or a space when we write numbers. How do the commas help make numbers easier to read?* (Students might say that it helps them to see the groups of three and how many groups of three there are. This idea will be further developed in Lesson 3 of this unit as students find that each place to the left is a larger power of ten.)

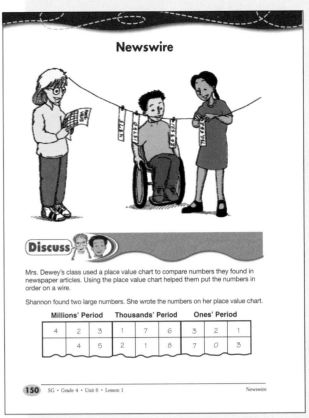

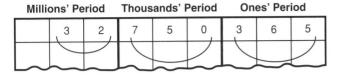

Newswire

(Discuss)

Mrs. Dewey's class used a place value chart to compare numbers they found in newspaper articles. Using the place value chart helped them put the numbers in order on a wire.

Shannon found two large numbers. She wrote the numbers on her place value chart.

Millions' Period			Thousands' Period			Ones' Period		
4	2	3	1	7	6	3	2	1
4	5	2	1	8	7	0	3

150 SG • Grade 4 • Unit 6 • Lesson 1   Newswire

Student Guide - page 150

Then she read the first number out loud, "Four hundred twenty-three million, one hundred seventy-six thousand, three hundred twenty-one." Shannon noticed that there is a repeating pattern. Can you describe the pattern?

Each repeating core pattern is called a **period** on the *Place Value Chart*.

* The first three-digit group on the right is the **ones' period.** It is made up of ones, tens, and hundreds.

* The second group is the **thousands' period.** It is made up of thousands, ten thousands, and hundred thousands.

* The third group is the **millions' period.** It is made up of millions, ten millions, and hundred millions.

When you say a number, you say each period just the way you do when you read a number in the ones' period and then you add the name of the period. For example, to read Shannon's second number, say, "Forty-five million, two hundred eighteen thousand, seven hundred three." When writing numbers, place a comma or a space between each period to make reading easier: 45,218,703.

Jacob found these numbers in the *National Parks Gazette*:

National Parks Numbers

Crater Lake in Oregon **183,224 acres**	Kobuk Valley National Park in Alaska **1,750,736 acres**	Glacier National Park in Montana **1,013,572 acres**	Canyonlands National Park in Utah **337,570 acres**	Voyageurs National Park in Minnesota **218,200 acres**
Extraordinary blue lake in crater of extinct volcano encircled by lava walls 500 to 2000 feet high.	Caribou and black bears; archaeological sites indicate that humans have lived there for more than 10,000 years.	Superb Rocky Mountain scenery; numerous glaciers, and glacial lakes.	At junction of Colorado and Green Rivers; extensive evidence of prehistoric Indians.	Abundant lakes, forests, wildlife, and canoeing.

Newswire   SG • Grade 4 • Unit 6 • Lesson 1 **151**

Student Guide - page 151

Student Guide - page 152 (Answers on p. 35)

Student Guide - page 153 (Answers on p. 35)

The problems on the *Newswire* Activity Pages in the *Student Guide* provide more practice in reading, writing, and ordering large numbers using National Parks as a context. Have students use the remaining rows on their copy of the *Place Value Chart* to list the number of acres for each National Park in order from smallest to largest.

Content Note

Acres. The questions in the *Student Guide* involve the areas of some national parks. These areas are given in acres. An acre is a measure of land equal to 43,560 square feet; there are 640 acres in a square mile. Students may be unfamiliar with this measurement. Help them visualize it by telling them that the playing area of a football field is a little larger than an acre.

Math Facts

- DPP Bit A begins the review and practice of the multiplication facts for the nines with the *Triangle Flash Cards*.

- Home Practice Part 1 reminds students to take home their flash cards and practice the multiplication facts for the nines.

Homework and Practice

- Assign the questions in the Homework section of the *Newswire* Activity Pages in the *Student Guide*. Students may use the *Place Value Chart* in the *Discovery Assignment Book* to order the numbers listed in the table in the Homework section. Students may continue to search at home for numbers in the news to contribute to the newswire.

- DPP Task B reviews 2- and 3-digit addition and subtraction. It also provides practice ordering large numbers.

- Assign Part 5 of the Home Practice. This exercise provides further practice ordering and writing large numbers.

Answers for Part 5 of the Home Practice are in the Answer Key at the end of this lesson and at the end of this unit.

Name _____ Date _____

Unit 6 Home Practice

PART 1 *Triangle Flash Cards: 9s*

Study for the quiz on the multiplication facts for the nines. Take home your *Triangle Flash Cards: 9s* and your list of facts you need to study.

Here's how to use the flash cards. Ask a family member to choose one flash card at a time. He or she should cover the corner containing the highest number. This number will be the answer to a multiplication fact. Multiply the two uncovered numbers.

Your teacher will tell you when the quiz on the 9s will be.

PART 2 **Mixed-Up Multiplication Tables**

1. Complete the table. Then, describe any patterns you see.

×	2	3	5	9	10
4					
6		18			
7					
8					

2. The letter *n* stands for a missing number. Find the missing number in each number sentence.

   A. $n \times 7 = 14$ B. $3 \times n = 24$ C. $n \times 4 = 16$ D. $n \times 8 = 80$

   E. $9 \times n = 63$ F. $n \times 8 = 64$ G. $4 \times n = 36$ H. $n \times 5 = 30$

PLACE VALUE PATTERNS   DAB • Grade 4 • Unit 6   **67**

Name _____ Date _____

PART 5 **Numbers in the News**

Keenya and Nicholas found the following numbers in the newspaper. Write the numbers in order from smallest to largest in the following place value chart.

4,130,243   7,931,435   39,905   793,027

4,613,378   9835   42,319

Millions			Thousands			Ones		

Write the smallest number in words.

Write the largest number in words.

PLACE VALUE PATTERNS   DAB • Grade 4 • Unit 6   **69**

Assessment

Use the *Observational Assessment Record* to record students' abilities to read and order large numbers.

Name _____ Date _____

Triangle Flash Cards: 9s

- Work with a partner. Each partner cuts out the flash cards below.
- Your partner chooses one card at a time and covers the shaded corner.
- Multiply the two uncovered numbers.
- Divide the cards into three piles: those facts you know and can answer quickly, those you can figure out with a strategy, and those you need to learn.
- Practice the last two piles again. Then make a list of the facts you need to practice at home.
- Repeat the directions for your partner.

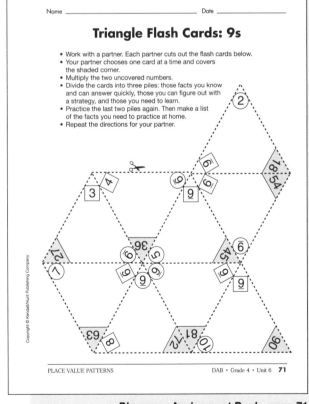

PLACE VALUE PATTERNS   DAB • Grade 4 • Unit 6   **71**

URG • Grade 4 • Unit 6 • Lesson 1   33

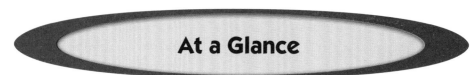
Math Facts and Daily Practice and Problems

DPP Bit A begins review and practice of the nines multiplication facts. Task B is an arithmetic review.

Before the Activity

Hang a wire accessible to the students. Cut index cards in half lengthwise. Prepare a bulletin board or blank wall.

Part 1. Constructing the Newswire

1. Student pairs search news articles for large numbers. They highlight four numbers and cut out the paragraphs. They copy the numbers onto the *Place Value Chart* in the *Discovery Assignment Book*. They also copy the numbers onto index card halves.
2. Students sort newspaper clippings into categories (Thousands, Ten Thousands, Hundred Thousands, and A Million or More) on a Newswire bulletin board.
3. Use the transparency of the *Place Value Chart* as a guide as students read and order large numbers.
4. Students identify the smallest and largest numbers. They record the numbers on the *Place Value Chart* transparency, read the numbers out loud, and place the numbers in order on the newswire.

Part 2. Investigating and Using Patterns in the *Place Value Chart*

Students discuss the pattern highlighted by the *Place Value Chart.* They practice reading, writing, and ordering large numbers using the *Newswire* Activity Pages in the *Student Guide.*

Homework

1. Assign the Homework section in the *Student Guide.* Students look for numbers in newspapers at home. They bring in the numbers and add them to the newswire.
2. Assign Parts 1 and 5 of the Home Practice.

Assessment

Use the *Observational Assessment Record* to note students' abilities to read and order large numbers.

Answer Key is on pages 35–36.

Notes:

Student Guide (p. 152)

I.

Millions			Thousands			Ones		
			1	8	3	2	2	4
			2	1	8	2	0	0
			3	3	7	5	7	0
		1	0	1	3	5	7	2
		1	7	5	0	7	3	6

one hundred eighty-three thousand, two hundred twenty-four

two hundred eighteen thousand, two hundred

three hundred thirty-seven thousand, five hundred seventy

one million, thirteen thousand, five hundred seventy-two

one million, seven hundred fifty thousand, seven hundred thirty-six

2. Glacier National Park

3. A. Canyonlands National Park

B. Kobuk Valley National Park

Student Guide (p. 153)

Homework

I. 801,163; eight hundred one thousand, one hundred sixty-three; 922,651; nine hundred twenty-two thousand, six hundred fifty-one; 2,219,791; two million, two hundred nineteen thousand, seven hundred ninety-one; 3,224,840; three million, two hundred twenty-four thousand, eight hundred forty; 7,523,898; seven million, five hundred twenty-three thousand, eight hundred ninety-eight.

2. Olympic National Park and Big Bend National Park

3.*

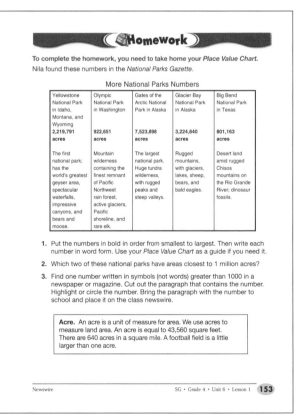

Student Guide - page 152

Student Guide - page 153

*Answers and/or discussion are included in the Lesson Guide.

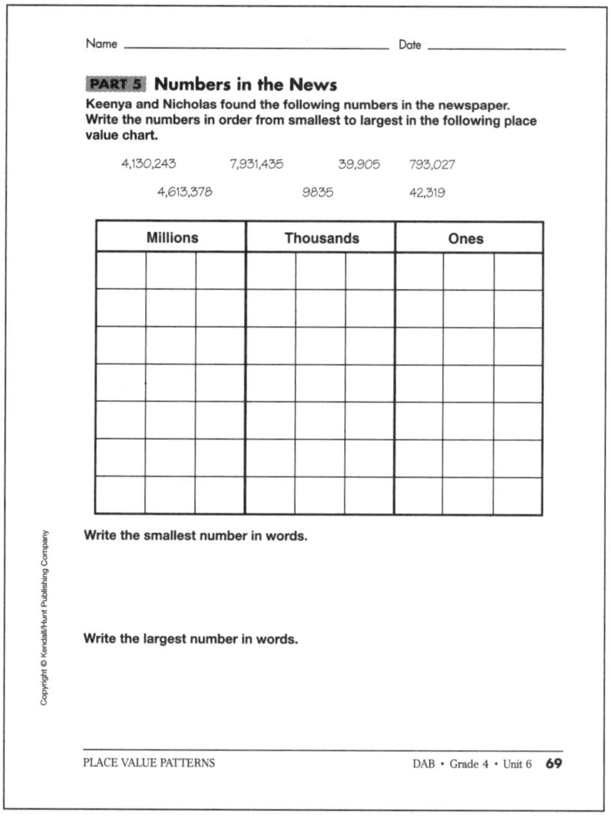

Name _____ Date _____

PART 5 **Numbers in the News**

Keenya and Nicholas found the following numbers in the newspaper.
Write the numbers in order from smallest to largest in the following place
value chart.

4,130,243   7,931,435   39,905   793,027

4,613,378   9835   42,319

Millions			Thousands			Ones		

Write the smallest number in words.

Write the largest number in words.

PLACE VALUE PATTERNS   DAB • Grade 4 • Unit 6 **69**

Discovery Assignment Book - page 69

Discovery Assignment Book (p. 69)

Home Practice*

Part 5. Numbers in the News

Millions			Thousands			Ones		
					9	8	3	5
				3	9	9	0	5
				4	2	3	1	9
			7	9	3	0	2	7
	4	1	3	0	2	4	3
	4	6	1	3	3	7	8
	7	9	3	1	4	3	5

nine thousand, eight hundred thirty-five

seven million, nine hundred thirty-one thousand,
four hundred thirty-five

*Answers for all the Home Practice in the *Discovery Assignment Book* are at the end of the unit.

Lesson 2

Doubles

Estimated Class Sessions

2-3

Lesson Overview

An old folktale serves as a context for investigating the patterns when numbers are doubled again and again. Students keep track of the doubling in a data table. They explore patterns and make predictions. Students analyze the data to make predictions.

Key Content

- Investigating large numbers.
- Using diagrams to solve problems.
- Using patterns in data tables to solve problems.
- Developing number sense for large numbers.

Key Vocabulary

- powers of two

Math Facts

DPP Bit C provides practice with the multiplication facts for the nines.

Homework

1. Assign the Homework section of the *Doubles* Activity Pages.
2. Assign Home Practice Part 2.

Assessment

1. Use DPP item D as an assessment.
2. Score homework *Question 1* using the Telling dimension of the *TIMS Multidimensional Rubric.*

Materials List

Supplies and Copies

Student	Teacher
Supplies for Each Student	**Supplies** • several colored pencils • 2 large sheets of paper, optional
Copies • 1 copy of *Three-column Data Table* per student, optional (*Unit Resource Guide* Page 47) • 1 copy of *Centimeter Graph Paper* per student (*Unit Resource Guide* Page 48)	**Copies/Transparencies** • 1 transparency of *Three-column Data Table*, optional (*Unit Resource Guide* Page 47) • 1 copy of *TIMS Multidimensional Rubric* (*Teacher Implementation Guide,* Assessment section) • 50 copies of *10,000 Sq Mm Grid*, optional (*Unit Resource Guide* Page 49)

All blackline masters including assessment, transparency, and DPP masters are also on the Teacher Resource CD.

Student Books

Doubles (*Student Guide* Pages 154–156)
Student Rubric: *Solving* (*Student Guide* Appendix B and Inside Back Cover)
Student Rubric: *Telling* (*Student Guide* Appendix C and Inside Back Cover)

Daily Practice and Problems and Home Practice

DPP items C–F (*Unit Resource Guide* Pages 16–18)
Home Practice Part 2 (*Discovery Assignment Book* Page 67)

Note: Classrooms whose pacing differs significantly from the suggested pacing of the units should use the Math Facts Calendar in Section 4 of the *Facts Resource Guide* to ensure students receive the complete math facts program.

Assessment Tools

TIMS Multidimensional Rubric (*Teacher Implementation Guide,* Assessment section)

Daily Practice and Problems

Suggestions for using the DPPs are on page 43.

C. Bit: Patterns (URG p. 16)

Complete:

$1 \times 9 =$

$2 \times 9 =$

$3 \times 9 =$

$4 \times 9 =$

$5 \times 9 =$

$6 \times 9 =$

$7 \times 9 =$

$8 \times 9 =$

$9 \times 9 =$

$10 \times 9 =$

What patterns do you see?

D. Task: The Long and the Short

(URG p. 17)

Write the following numbers in words:

A. 421   B. 8536

C. 58,972   D. 20,380

Write the following words as numbers:

E. six thousand nineteen

F. two thousand, three hundred forty-one

G. two hundred one thousand, five hundred two

E. Bit: Median and Mean

(URG p. 17)

Ming experimented with 3 kinds of balls to find out which one bounced highest. He dropped each type of ball five times from 1 meter.

Here are the bounce heights for the tennis ball: 52 cm, 47 cm, 55 cm, 52 cm, and 50 cm.

1. Find the median bounce height.
2. Use a calculator to find the mean bounce height to the nearest cm.

F. Task: The Mystery Unfolds

(URG p. 18)

1. Fold a sheet of paper in half. Now unfold it. How many sections are there?
2. Fold the paper in half again. This time without unfolding, fold it in half once more. Now unfold it. How many sections are there?
3. Complete the following data table by folding your paper in half 3, 4, and 5 times:

Number of Folds	Number of Sections	Number of Sections Written with Exponents
1	2	2^1
2		2^2
3		

4. What patterns do you see?
5. Predict the number of sections after the paper has been folded in half 6 times.

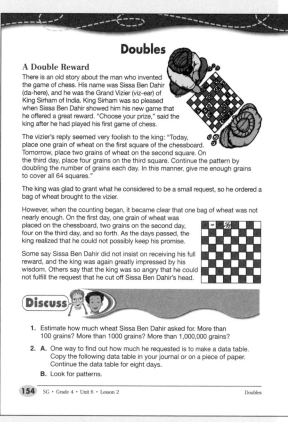

Doubles

A Double Reward

There is an old story about the man who invented the game of chess. His name was Sissa Ben Dahir (da-here), and he was the Grand Vizier (viz-ear) of King Sirham of India. King Sirham was so pleased when Sissa Ben Dahir showed him his new game that he offered a great reward. "Choose your prize," said the king after he had played his first game of chess.

The vizier's reply seemed very foolish to the king: "Today, place one grain of wheat on the first square of the chessboard. Tomorrow, place two grains of wheat on the second square. On the third day, place four grains on the third square. Continue the pattern by doubling the number of grains each day. In this manner, give me enough grains to cover all 64 squares."

The king was glad to grant what he considered to be a small request, so he ordered a bag of wheat brought to the vizier.

However, when the counting began, it became clear that one bag of wheat was not nearly enough. On the first day, one grain of wheat was placed on the chessboard, two grains on the second day, four on the third day, and so forth. As the days passed, the king realized that he could not possibly keep his promise.

Some say Sissa Ben Dahir did not insist on receiving his full reward, and the king was again greatly impressed by his wisdom. Others say that the king was so angry that he could not fulfill the request that he cut off Sissa Ben Dahir's head.

Discuss

1. Estimate how much wheat Sissa Ben Dahir asked for. More than 100 grains? More than 1000 grains? More than 1,000,000 grains?

2. **A.** One way to find out how much he requested is to make a data table. Copy the following data table in your journal or on a piece of paper. Continue the data table for eight days.

   B. Look for patterns.

154   SG • Grade 4 • Unit 6 • Lesson 2   Doubles

Student Guide - page 154 (Answers on p. 50)

Content Note

Notes on Four-Function Calculators. Students can use calculators with a constant function to help them find powers of two quickly. Pressing

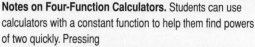

$$2 \times 2 = = = =$$

on most four-function calculators will continuously double numbers and produce the powers of two. Care must be taken to count the number of 2s correctly as shown in the following chart:

Power of Two	Keystrokes	Display
2^2	$2 \times 2 =$	4
2^3	$2 \times 2 = =$	8
2^4	$2 \times 2 = = =$	16

Notes on Scientific Calculators. If you have any scientific calculators available, you can find the powers of two easily by using the exponent key. Exponent keys are labeled differently on different scientific calculators. Possible labels include: $\wedge$ x^y y^x

To find 2^{20} press 2 y^x 20 $=$.
The result is 1,048,576. Note that 2^{64} is too large to fit in the display, so the answer is given in scientific notation. All of the digits cannot be shown in the calculator window. A good estimate for the actual answer is 18,447,000,000,000,000,000 (18 quintillion, 447 quadrillion). You may wish to borrow scientific calculators from a fifth-grade class.

Teaching the Activity

Introduce the activity by reading the *Doubles* Activity Pages in the *Student Guide.* These pages tell the story of Sissa Ben Dahir of India, who invented the game of chess. As a reward, he requested one grain of wheat on the first square of the chessboard on the first day, two grains on the second square on the second day, four grains on the third day, eight grains on the fourth, doubling the quantity each day until all 64 squares had been covered.

Content Note

Grand Vizier (vi-zer') is a title given to high political officers in the former Turkish Empire and in Muslim countries.

Question 1 asks students to estimate how much wheat the inventor will receive if his request is granted. This problem will be explored in several ways throughout the unit. (See the Daily Practice and Problems items F and N.) An intelligent guess is all that is asked for at this point.

Question 2A asks students to begin a doubling data table and look for patterns. They may use a *Three-column Data Table*. Figure 5 shows a data table completed for eight days. Point out that the numbers in the second column are called **powers of two.** Remind students of their work with exponents in Unit 4.

Doubling Data Table

D Time in Days	N Number of Grains of Wheat Added	T Total Number of Grains of Wheat
1	1	1
2	$2^1 = 2$	3
3	$2 \times 2 = 2^2 = 4$	7
4	$2 \times 2 \times 2 = 2^3 = 8$	15
5	$2 \times 2 \times 2 \times 2 = 2^4 = 16$	31
6	$2 \times 2 \times 2 \times 2 \times 2 = 2^5 = 32$	63
7	$2 \times 2 \times 2 \times 2 \times 2 \times 2 = 2^6 = 64$	127
8	$2^7 = 128$	255

Figure 5: *A completed data table for eight days*

Question 3 asks students to describe the patterns they see. Possible patterns are:

- The number of grains of wheat added (N) doubles each day.

- After the first few days, the total number of grains of wheat quickly adds up.

- The total number of grains of wheat (T) is always an odd number.

- The exponent in the second column is one less than the number of days (D).

- The total number (T) in any row is one less than the number added (N) in the following row.

- The total number of grains of wheat on a given day is one less than twice the number of grains added. For example, on day 4 the number of grains of wheat added was 8; $8 \times 2 \times 1 = 15$. The total number of grains in all on Day 4 is 15.

Students can use the patterns and their calculators to answer *Question 4*. Or students can compute the table until Day 18. The number of grains of wheat added on the eighteenth day is 2^{17} or 131,072 and the total number is $2 \times 131{,}072 - 1 = 262{,}143$.

Question 5 asks students to predict when the total number of grains of wheat on the chessboard will reach 1,000,000. Students should first make a guess, then look for patterns in the data and use the data to revise the estimates. You may wish to restate the problem:

- *On what day will 1,000,000 grains of wheat be collected?*

Students should record their predictions in their journals or on their data tables. Ask students to share their predictions and explain their thinking. Discuss several different predictions without giving any clues about what will happen.

To check their predictions *(Question 6)*, students can continue filling in the data table until the total number of grains (T) is greater than 1,000,000. Or students can use the constant function on their calculators and use the patterns in the table to check their predictions. When wheat is added on the twentieth day ($D = 20$), the total number of grains of wheat (T) will be more than 1,000,000. (When $D = 20$, $N = 2^{19}$ or 524,288 and $T = 1{,}048{,}575$.)

At this point you can read one of the versions of the story recommended in the Literature Connections.

Writing numbers using exponents in the second column may help you see more patterns. Each of the numbers in the second column of the data table are **powers of two.** For example, $2 \times 2 \times 2 = 2^3$ is read "two to the third power." We say that 2^3 is the "third power of two." Follow the examples to write the powers of two, using exponents in your data table. Use a calculator to help you. (*Hint:* You may need to stop writing $2 \times 2 \times 2 \ldots$ after several rows.)

Doubling Data Table

D Time in Days	N Number of Grains of Wheat Added	T Total Number of Grains of Wheat
1	1	1
2	$2 \times 1 = 2$	3
3	$2 \times 2 = 2^2 = 4$	7
4	$2 \times 2 \times 2 = 2^3 = 8$	15

3. Describe any patterns you see.

4. **A.** How many grains of wheat will be added on the eighteenth day?
   B. How many total grains of wheat are needed by the eighteenth day?

5. Use the patterns to help you predict when the total number of grains of wheat on the chessboard will reach 1 million.

6. Check your prediction. Continue your data table until the total number of grains of wheat reaches a million.

7. Make a point graph for the first two columns in your data table on *Centimeter Graph Paper.* Put the time in days (D) on the horizontal axis. Scale the horizontal axis by ones. Put the number of grains of wheat added each day (N) on the vertical axis. Scale the vertical axis by fours.
   A. Do the points form a straight line? If so, draw a best-fit line through the points.
   B. If the points do not form a line, describe the shape of the graph.

Doubles   SG · Grade 4 · Unit 6 · Lesson 2   **155**

Student Guide - page 155 (Answers on p. 50)

TIMS Tip

There are other ways to organize the data table. It may help students to use a four-column data table with headings as shown below. Students may see more patterns if they include a separate column for the previous day's total (P) and write number sentences that show the sum of the number of grains added (N) and the previous day's total (P).

D Time in Days	N Number of Grains of Wheat Added	P Previous Day's Total	T Total Grains of Wheat N + P = Total
1	1	0	$1 + 0 = 1$
2	2	1	$2 + 1 = 3$
3	$2 \times 2 = 2^2 = 4$	3	$4 + 3 = 7$
4	$2 \times 2 \times 2 = 2^3 = 8$	7	$8 + 7 = 15$
5	$2 \times 2 \times 2 \times 2 = 2^4 = 16$	15	$16 + 15 = 31$
6	$2 \times 2 \times 2 \times 2 \times 2 = 2^5 = 32$	31	$32 + 31 = 63$
7	$2 \times 2 \times 2 \times 2 \times 2 \times 2 = 2^6 = 64$	63	$64 + 63 = 127$
8	$2^7 = 128$	127	$128 + 127 = 255$

Stories. There are many versions of the story told in the *Doubles Activity Pages* in the *Student Guide* about the grains of wheat on the chessboard. Two good resources for the story are Chapter 1 of *One, Two, Three . . . Infinity* by George Gamow and "Pastimes of Past and Present Times" in Volume Four of *The World of Mathematics* edited by James R. Newman. For complete references for these books, see the References Section of the Background for this unit. Two other versions for children are described in the Literature Connections for this lesson.

To fulfill his promise, the king needed $2^{64} - 1$ or 18,446,744,073,709,551,615 grains of wheat. This is eighteen quintillion, four hundred forty-six quadrillion, seven hundred forty-four trillion, seventy-three billion, seven hundred nine million, five hundred fifty-one thousand, six hundred fifteen grains of wheat. According to James Newman this is "enough to cover the surface of the earth to the depth of the twentieth part of a cubit." (One twentieth of a cubit is about one inch.)

Question 7 asks students to make a point graph by graphing the number of days (D) on the horizontal axis and the number of grains of wheat added each day (N) on the vertical axis. Students should see that as the number of days gets larger, the number of grains added gets much larger. The points form a curve. When you discuss the question, show students how to sketch the curve using the points on the graph. Encourage students to tell a story for their graph. A sample graph is shown in Figure 6.

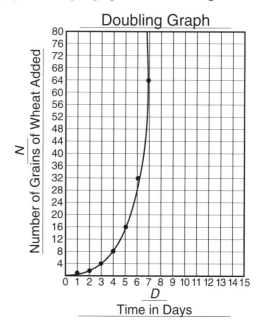

Figure 6: *A sample graph*

Math Facts

- DPP Bit C asks students to find the patterns in the multiplication facts for the nines.
- Part 2 of the Home Practice asks students to complete a multiplication table and use facts to solve problems with unknowns.

Homework and Practice

- The homework questions ask students to apply the doubling patterns to other problems.
- Bit E reviews mean and median. Task F provides a doubling problem that uses the same skills as the problem in the lesson.
- Assign Part 2 of the Home Practice for homework.

Answers for Part 2 of the Home Practice are in the Answer Key at the end of this lesson and at the end of this unit.

Assessment

- Use DPP item D as an assessment of students' abilities to read and write large numbers.
- Use the Telling dimension of the *TIMS Multidimensional Rubric* to score students' responses to **Question 1** in the Homework section.

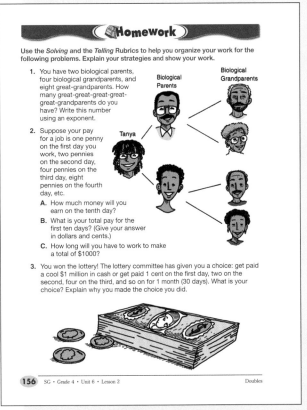

Homework

Use the *Solving* and the *Telling* Rubrics to help you organize your work for the following problems. Explain your strategies and show your work.

1. You have two biological parents, four biological grandparents, and eight great-grandparents. How many great-great-great-great-great-grandparents do you have? Write this number using an exponent.

   Biological Parents

   Biological Grandparents

   Tanya

2. Suppose your pay for a job is one penny on the first day you work, two pennies on the second day, four pennies on the third day, eight pennies on the fourth day, etc.
   A. How much money will you earn on the tenth day?
   B. What is your total pay for the first ten days? (Give your answer in dollars and cents.)
   C. How long will you have to work to make a total of $1000?

3. You won the lottery! The lottery committee has given you a choice: get paid a cool $1 million in cash or get paid 1 cent on the first day, two on the second, four on the third, and so on for 1 month (30 days). What is your choice? Explain why you made the choice you did.

156   SG • Grade 4 • Unit 6 • Lesson 2   Doubles

Student Guide - page 156 (Answers on p. 51)

Name _____ Date _____

Unit 6 Home Practice

PART 1 Triangle Flash Cards: 9s
Study for the quiz on the multiplication facts for the nines. Take home your *Triangle Flash Cards: 9s* and your list of facts you need to study.

Here's how to use the flash cards. Ask a family member to choose one flash card at a time. He or she should cover the corner containing the highest number. This number will be the answer to a multiplication fact. Multiply the two uncovered numbers.

Your teacher will tell you when the quiz on the 9s will be.

PART 2 Mixed-Up Multiplication Tables

1. Complete the table. Then, describe any patterns you see.

×	2	3	5	9	10
4					
6		18			
7					
8					

2. The letter *n* stands for a missing number. Find the missing number in each number sentence.
   A. $n \times 7 = 14$ B. $3 \times n = 24$ C. $n \times 4 = 16$ D. $n \times 8 = 80$
   E. $9 \times n = 63$ F. $n \times 8 = 64$ G. $4 \times n = 36$ H. $n \times 5 = 30$

PLACE VALUE PATTERNS   DAB • Grade 4 • Unit 6 **67**

Discovery Assignment Book - page 67 (Answers on p. 51)

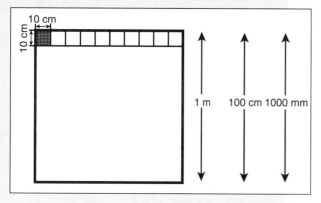

Figure 7: *Square meter grid*

This extension activity creates a visual image of the doubling process. You can use it as students are filling in their data tables or after they complete the questions in the *Student Guide.* Mark a square meter on a large piece of paper and use 50 copies of the *10,000 Sq Mm Grid* Blackline Master to prepare one hundred sq mm grids. Glue one 10,000 sq mm grid in the upper left-hand corner as shown in Figure 7. (You will add more grids as they are filled.) Hang this paper in a place convenient for a student to reach.

Show students the square meter displayed in the room. Describe how each side of the square meter measures 1000 millimeters. Tell students that each square millimeter stands for one grain of wheat. Explain that there are 1,000,000 sq mm in the square meter ($1000 \times 1000 = 1,000,000$).

Ask a student to color in the first sq mm on the meter square using a sharpened color pencil. Ask a second student to color 2 sq mm and enter the data in the data table or they can refer to the Doubling Data Table they just completed. Ask a third student to color in 4 sq mm. Continue this procedure, asking each student to double the number that the previous student colored. These numbers are recorded in the second column (Number of Grains of Wheat Added) of the Doubling Data Table. Students should color in consecutive squares. When necessary, add another 10,000 sq mm grid to the square. Predict the number of students it will take to fill the square meter (color 1,000,000 sq mm).

As numbers become larger, suggest that students develop a strategy for coloring in square millimeters. One way to think about this is that each 10,000 sq mm grid measures 10 cm or 100 mm on a side as shown in Figure 8. This means that there are 100 rows, each with 100 sq mm. The 10,000 sq mm grid is also divided into square centimeters. Each square centimeter is made up of 100 sq mm (10 mm by 10 mm). Students can count by 100s as they color. For each 100 sq mm, they can color 1 row on the 10,000 mm grid or 1 sq cm. As they color in the larger numbers, they should switch to crayons.

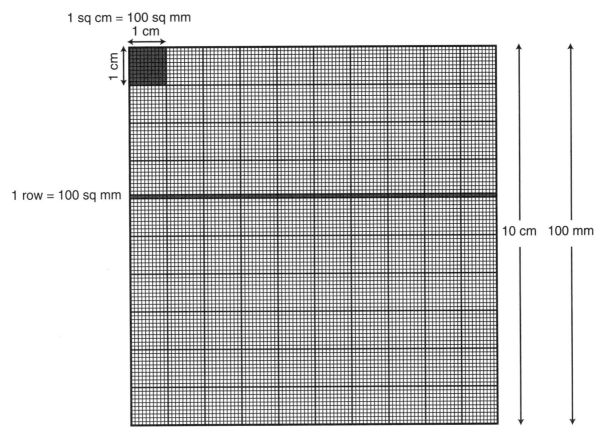

Figure 8: *10,000 sq mm grid: 100 rows with 100 square mm per row*

Literature Connections

- *The King's Chessboard* by David Birch. The story of the doubling of rice on the chessboard is retold in a different way. The rice is measured in ounces, pounds, and tons.

- *A Grain of Rice* by Helena Clare Pittman. This is a Chinese version of the story of a reward of doubling grains of rice. In this tale, a young man wins the hand of the emperor's daughter through hard work and cleverness.

Journal Prompt

Students can read other versions of the story and report to the class. How are the stories alike? How are they different?

At a Glance

Math Facts and Daily Practice and Problems

DPP Bit C provides practice with the multiplication facts for the nines. Bit E reviews mean and median. Task F is a doubling problem similar to the problem in the lesson.

Teaching the Activity

1. Students read the *Doubles* Activity Pages in the *Student Guide*.
2. Students discuss the questions and begin a data table as shown in the *Student Guide*.
3. Students find patterns in the data table and describe them.
4. Students use the patterns to solve problems.
5. Students graph their data and explore the shape of the graph.
6. Read one of the stories listed in the Literature Connections (optional).

Homework

1. Assign the Homework section of the *Doubles* Activity Pages.
2. Assign Home Practice Part 2.

Assessment

1. Use DPP item D as an assessment.
2. Score homework **Question 1** using the Telling dimension of the *TIMS Multidimensional Rubric*.

Extension

Create a visual image of the doubling process using 50 copies of the *10,000 Sq Mm Grid*.

Connection

Share *The King's Chessboard* or *A Grain of Rice*. Both stories show doubling.

Answer Key is on pages 50–51.

Notes:

Name _____   Date _____

_____

Name _____ Date _____

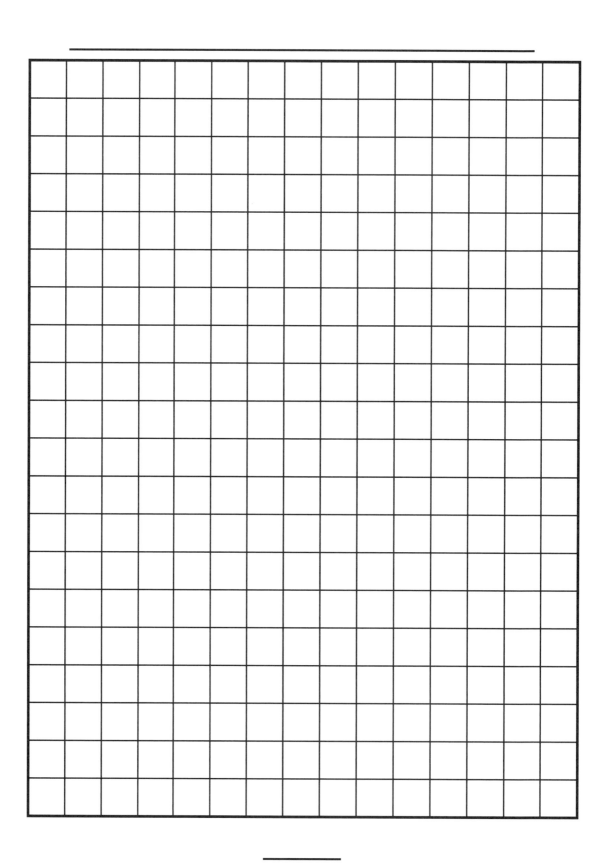

Centimeter Graph Paper, Blackline Master

10,000 Sq Mm Grid

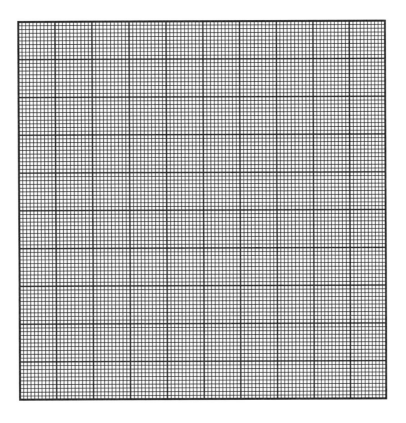

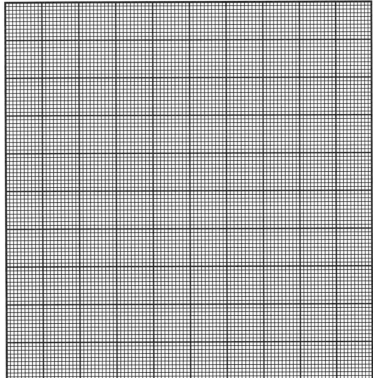

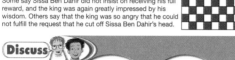

Doubles

A Double Reward

There is an old story about the man who invented the game of chess. His name was Sissa Ben Dahir (da-here), and he was the Grand Vizier (viz-ear) of King Sirham of India. King Sirham was so pleased when Sissa Ben Dahir showed him his new game that he offered a great reward. "Choose your prize," said the king after he had played his first game of chess.

The vizier's reply seemed very foolish to the king: "Today, place one grain of wheat on the first square of the chessboard. Tomorrow, place two grains of wheat on the second square. On the third day, place four grains on the third square. Continue the pattern by doubling the number of grains each day. In this manner, give me enough grains to cover all 64 squares."

The king was glad to grant what he considered to be a small request, so he ordered a bag of wheat brought to the vizier.

However, when the counting began, it became clear that one bag of wheat was not nearly enough. On the first day, one grain of wheat was placed on the chessboard, two grains on the second day, four on the third day, and so forth. As the days passed, the king realized that he could not possibly keep his promise.

Some say Sissa Ben Dahir did not insist on receiving his full reward, and the king was again greatly impressed by his wisdom. Others say that the king was so angry that he could not fulfill the request that he cut off Sissa Ben Dahir's head.

Discuss

1. Estimate how much wheat Sissa Ben Dahir asked for. More than 100 grains? More than 1000 grains? More than 1,000,000 grains?

2. **A.** One way to find out how much he requested is to make a data table. Copy the following data table in your journal or on a piece of paper. Continue the data table for eight days.

   B. Look for patterns.

154 SG • Grade 4 • Unit 6 • Lesson 2   Doubles

Student Guide - page 154

Writing numbers using exponents in the second column may help you see more patterns. Each of the numbers in the second column of the data table are **powers of two.** For example, $2 \times 2 \times 2 = 2^3$ is read "two to the third power." We say that 2^3 is the "third power of two." Follow the examples to write the powers of two, using exponents in your data table. Use a calculator to help you. (*Hint:* You may need to stop writing $2 \times 2 \times 2 \ldots$ after several rows.)

Doubling Data Table

D Time in Days	N Number of Grains of Wheat Added	T Total Number of Grains of Wheat
1	1	1
2	$2 \times 1 = 2$	3
3	$2 \times 2 = 2^2 = 4$	7
4	$2 \times 2 \times 2 = 2^3 = 8$	15

3. Describe any patterns you see.

4. **A.** How many grains of wheat will be added on the eighteenth day?
   B. How many total grains of wheat are needed by the eighteenth day?

5. Use the patterns to help you predict when the total number of grains of wheat on the chessboard will reach 1 million.

6. Check your prediction. Continue your data table until the total number of grains of wheat reaches a million.

7. Make a point graph for the first two columns in your data table on *Centimeter Graph Paper*. Put the time in days (*D*) on the horizontal axis. Scale the horizontal axis by ones. Put the number of grains of wheat added each day (*N*) on the vertical axis. Scale the vertical axis by fours.

   A. Do the points form a straight line? If so, draw a best-fit line through the points.

   B. If the points do not form a line, describe the shape of the graph.

Doubles   SG • Grade 4 • Unit 6 • Lesson 2 **155**

Student Guide - page 155

Student Guide (pp. 154–155)

Doubles

1. Estimates will vary.

2.* **A.–B.** See data table in Figure 5 of Lesson Guide 2.

3. Descriptions will vary. Some possible patterns include: the number of grains of wheat added each day doubles each day; the total number of grains of wheat grows very quickly; the exponent in the second column is one less than the number of days; and the total number (*T*) in any row is one less than the number added (*N*) in the following row.*

4.* **A.** 131,072   5. Predictions will vary.*
   B. 262,143

6. Total number of grains of wheat will reach 1,000,000 on Day 20.*

Doubling Data Table

D Time in Days	N Number of Grains of Wheat Added	T Total Number of Grains of Wheat
1	1	1
2	$2^1 = 2$	3
3	$2 \times 2 = 2^2 = 4$	7
4	$2 \times 2 \times 2 = 2^3 = 8$	15
5	$2 \times 2 \times 2 \times 2 = 2^4 = 16$	31
6	$2 \times 2 \times 2 \times 2 \times 2 = 2^5 = 32$	63
7	$2 \times 2 \times 2 \times 2 \times 2 \times 2 = 2^6 = 64$	127
8	$2^7 = 128$	255
9	$2^8 = 256$	511
10	$2^9 = 512$	1023
11	$2^{10} = 1024$	2047
12	$2^{11} = 2048$	4095
13	$2^{12} = 4096$	8191
14	$2^{13} = 8192$	16,383
15	$2^{14} = 16,384$	32,767
16	$2^{15} = 32,768$	65,535
17	$2^{16} = 65,536$	131,071
18	$2^{17} = 131,072$	262,143
19	$2^{18} = 262,144$	524,287
20	$2^{19} = 524,288$	1,048,575
21	$2^{20} = 1,048,576$	2,097,151

7.* See Figure 6 in Lesson Guide 2.
   A. No.
   B. Descriptions will vary. Students should see that the points fall on a curve or that the points tend to go uphill slowly at first, then very quickly.

---

*Answers and/or discussion are included in the Lesson Guide.

Student Guide (p. 156)

Homework

1. $2^7 = 128$ great-great-great-great-great-grandparents. Strategies will vary.

2. **A.** $5.12

   B. $10.23

   C. 17 days; $1310.71

3. Answers will vary. Taking one cent on the first day, two on the second, four on the third, etc., will give you more money, but you'll have to wait longer to accumulate it. This is the same problem as the one described in the story of doubling grains of wheat. Following the same pattern, on the 20th day you will have received a total of $10,485.75 with the doubling option. On the 27th day, you will have received more than one million dollars. On the 30th day you will have more than ten million dollars.

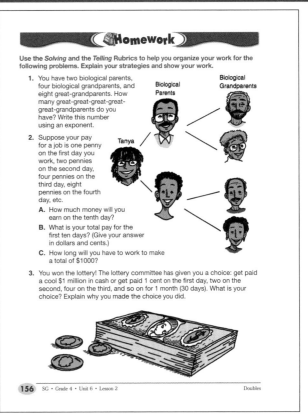

Student Guide - page 156

Discovery Assignment Book (p. 67)

Home Practice*

Part 2. Mixed-Up Multiplication Tables

1.

×	2	3	5	9	10
4	8	12	20	36	40
6	12	18	30	54	60
7	14	21	35	63	70
8	16	24	40	72	80

Patterns will vary.

2. **A.** 2   **B.** 8

   C. 4   **D.** 10

   E. 7   **F.** 8

   G. 9   **H.** 6

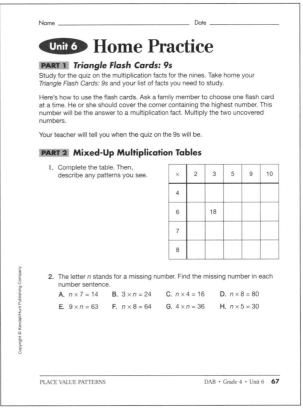

Discovery Assignment Book - page 67

*Answers for all the Home Practice in the *Discovery Assignment Book* are at the end of the unit.

Lesson 3

Big Base-Ten Pieces

Lesson Overview

Estimated Class Sessions
2-3

Students construct proportional base-ten models for ten thousand, one hundred thousand, and one million based on the familiar size and shape relationships of the base-ten pieces. These conceptual models help students visualize the powers of ten patterns in our place value system.

Key Content

- Representing large numbers (to 1 million) with base-ten pieces.
- Linking the powers of 10 to the place value system.
- Understanding place value (to the millions).
- Translating between different representations of large numbers (concrete, pictorial, symbolic).
- Developing number sense for large numbers (to the millions).

Key Vocabulary

- megabit
- period
- place value
- super bit
- super flat
- super skinny

Math Facts

DPP items G, H, and J provide practice with math facts.

Homework

1. Students play the game *Draw, Place, and Read* at home.
2. Assign Home Practice Part 3.

Assessment

Use the Journal Prompt as an assessment.

Curriculum Sequence

Before This Unit

Place Value

Students reviewed place value to the thousands using base-ten pieces in Unit 3.

After This Unit

Place Value

Students will use place value concepts as they develop paper-and-pencil procedures for multiplication and division in Units 7 and 11. They will also revisit place value and large numbers in Grade 5 Unit 2.

Materials List

Supplies and Copies

Student	Teacher
Supplies for Each Student Group • meterstick • masking tape	**Supplies** • 24 metersticks • masking tape • 6–16 base-ten packs • 4–8 rulers • paper for covering the big base-ten pieces, optional
Copies • 1 copy of *Digit Cards 0–9* per student group copied back to back (*Unit Resource Guide* Pages 61–62)	**Copies/Transparencies** • 1 transparency of *Place Value Chart II* (*Unit Resource Guide* Page 63)

All blackline masters including assessment, transparency, and DPP masters are also on the Teacher Resource CD.

Student Books

Big Base-Ten Pieces (*Student Guide* Pages 157–159)
Draw, Place, and Read (*Discovery Assignment Book* Page 75)

Daily Practice and Problems and Home Practice

DPP items G–J (*Unit Resource Guide* Pages 19–20)
Home Practice Part 3 (*Discovery Assignment Book* Page 68)

Note: Classrooms whose pacing differs significantly from the suggested pacing of the units should use the Math Facts Calendar in Section 4 of the *Facts Resource Guide* to ensure students receive the complete math facts program.

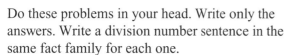

Daily Practice and Problems

Suggestions for using the DPPs are on page 59.

G. Bit: Nines Are Fine (URG p. 19)

Do these problems in your head. Write only the answers. Write a division number sentence in the same fact family for each one.

A. $9 \times 5 =$ B. $9 \times 7 =$
C. $8 \times 9 =$ D. $9 \times 2 =$
E. $6 \times 9 =$ F. $9 \times 4 =$
G. $10 \times 9 =$ H. $9 \times 9 =$
I. $9 \times 3 =$ J. $1 \times 9 =$

I. Bit: Ana's Purchase (URG p. 20)

1. Ana bought a gallon of milk for $2.49, a box of crackers for $1.56, and a magazine for $2.95. Will $10.00 be enough to pay the bill?
2. About how much change will Ana get back?

H. Task: Calculator Counting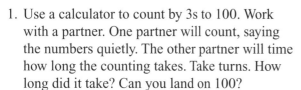
   (URG p. 19)

1. Use a calculator to count by 3s to 100. Work with a partner. One partner will count, saying the numbers quietly. The other partner will time how long the counting takes. Take turns. How long did it take? Can you land on 100?
2. Use the data from Question 1 to predict how long it would take to count by 9s to 100. Then, use a calculator to count by 9s to 100. How long did it take? Can you land on 100?

J. Task: Mr. and Mrs. Head (URG p. 20)

Mr. Head says that $9 \times 5 = 46$, and Mrs. Head cannot convince him he's wrong. Write a letter to Mr. Head explaining what 9×5 equals and why. You may use drawings in your letter.

Collect the metersticks and packs you will need. Cut large sheets of paper for covering the models.

Teaching the Activity

This activity is divided into two parts. The first part is teacher-led with the class building a set of big base-ten pieces. In the second part, students use the *Big Base-Ten Pieces* Activity Pages in the *Student Guide* to become more familiar with the place value chart and use exponents to represent powers of ten. When students are comfortable with the chart, they play a game called *Draw, Place, and Read*.

Part 1 Big Base-Ten Pieces

Discuss the size relationship of the base-ten pieces. Use the following discussion prompts and *Place Value Chart II* Transparency Master:

- Show a bit and a skinny. Ask students how many bits make a skinny. Students should respond that 10 bits make a skinny; a bit represents 1 and a skinny represents 10. If they are unclear, allow students to line up bits until they are the same length as a skinny. Since a skinny is 10 times the length of a bit, record 10×1 (ten groups of one) on your place value chart. See Figure 9.

- Show a skinny and a flat. Ask students how many skinnies make a flat. Students can see that 10 skinnies will make one flat. Record 10×10 (ten groups of ten) on the place value chart to show this relationship. Ask students to count by tens as you place ten skinnies together to make a flat. (10, 20, 30 . . . 100)

- Show a flat and a pack. Ask students how many flats make a pack. Students should again see the 10 times relationship between the flat and the pack. Students can count by hundreds as you place 10 flats on top of each other to make a pack (100, 200, 300, . . . 1000). Record 10×100 (ten groups of 100) on the place value chart.

- Ask, *"Which of the four kinds of base-ten pieces (bit, skinny, flat, pack) have the same shape?"*

  Students can see that the bit and the pack are both cubes. Tell students that since the bit and pack have the same shape, for this activity you are going to call the pack a **super bit.**

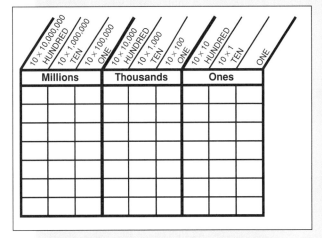

Figure 9: *A place value chart with the ten times relationship between places added*

TIMS Tip

To involve students in the construction of the big base-ten pieces, the class can build more than one super skinny and super flat. If supplies are available, have three groups build a super skinny, two groups build a super flat, and one group build a megabit. Groups who finish their super skinnies and super flats early can help the final group complete the megabit.

- *How can we follow the pattern in the place value chart and use the base-ten pieces to build a model of 10,000?*

A student will likely suggest that ten packs taped together in the shape of a skinny will show 10,000. If they do not, repeat the demonstration showing how ten bits connected together to make a rod make a skinny. Have students count by thousands as the ten packs are placed together to form a large rod. Demonstrate how ten packs fit the length of a meterstick as you move one pack from one end to the other.

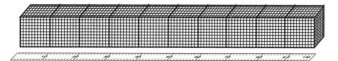

Figure 10: *Ten packs in a line*

After this demonstration, you and the students can construct a physical model of 10,000. You will need two packs and four metersticks. Place the packs 1 meter apart on a table or on the floor. Use the four metersticks to make the edges of your model by placing two of the sticks from pack to pack on the top and two of the sticks from pack to pack on the bottom. Tape the sticks in place and, if possible, cover your model with paper so that it more closely resembles the other base-ten pieces. See Figure 11. Name this model a **super skinny.**

Figure 11: *A super skinny constructed with two packs and four metersticks*

Ask:

- *What is the value of a super bit?* (1000)
- *How many super bits make a super skinny?* (10)
- *What is the value of a super skinny?* (10,000)

Record the 10 × 1000 relationship on the *Place Value Chart II* as shown in Figure 9. Call attention to the two patterns that are evolving. The first pattern is the shapes: **bit** (one), **skinny** (ten), **flat** (100), **super bit** (1000), **super skinny** (ten thousand). The second pattern is that each number is 10 times larger than the number to its right.

As you move to the left on the *Place Value Chart II*, ask:

- *What place comes next?* (100,000)
- *Ten times what number will equal 100,000?* (10,000. Again, emphasize the pattern of 10 times the number to the right.)
- *What shape model will continue the pattern of the base-ten pieces?* (a super flat)
- *How should we build this model?*

Guide students to see that 10 of the super skinnies will make a super flat. Have students count by 10,000s to 100,000 as you use your hands to pantomime pushing 10 super skinnies together.

With the students, build a model using four packs and eight metersticks. Lay down four metersticks to form a square. Place one pack in each corner of the square and tape the meterstick and packs together. Students can help you place the other four metersticks along the top edges to form a square. Tape these in place. If possible, cover the model with paper so it resembles a flat. Emphasize that the **super flat** model represents 10 super skinnies or 100 packs, just as the flat represents 10 skinnies or 100 bits. See Figure 12.

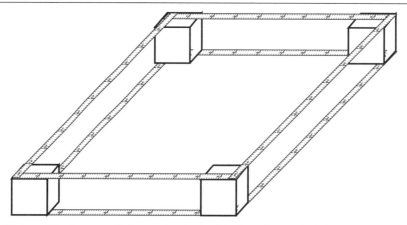

Figure 12: *A super flat constructed with 4 packs and eight metersticks*

Return to the *Place Value Chart II* and record
10 × 10,000 in the Hundred Thousand column. Ask:

- *What number comes next on the place value chart?* (1 million)
- *What number times 10 will equal 1,000,000?* (100,000)

Record 10 × 100,000 in the One Million column.
Emphasize the pattern of 10 times the number to the
right. See if students can identify the shape of the
model that will continue the pattern of the models of
the base-ten pieces. If students are not able to identify
the cube, go back to the ones' cube and name each
shape as you move through the place value chart (bit,
skinny, flat) until they are able to identify the shape as
a bit (cube). Name this model a **megabit.**

Guide students to see that ten of the super flats
stacked will make a megabit that is a cube that measures 1 meter × 1 meter × 1 meter. Have students
count by 100,000s to 1 million as you use your
hands to pretend to stack 10 super flats. To build this
model, you need 12 metersticks. Have students help
in constructing the megabit by holding the sticks in
place as someone tapes them together. To construct
this cube, place four metersticks on the floor in a
square. Use four more metersticks to build the edges
of the sides by placing one meterstick perpendicular
at each corner. Use tape to hold these sticks together.
You can use rulers to brace each corner on the bottom of the megabit. Now place the last four sticks in
a square on top of the four "sides." Use tape to hold
these together. If possible, cover the megabit with
paper. See Figure 13.

Part 2 Patterns in the Base-Ten Pieces

After building the physical models of the base-ten
pieces, turn to *Big Base-Ten Pieces* Activity Pages in
the *Student Guide.* Look at the opening artwork and
read the thoughts of the little mouse. Discuss why the
mouse prefers a megabit to the other models. Refer to
your models as you discuss the patterns in the shapes
and sizes of the pieces. *Question 1* asks students to
describe the patterns they see in the shapes. Beginning
with the bit, the shapes repeat: bit, skinny, flat, bit,
skinny, flat, bit.

Question 2 asks students to look for a pattern in
the sizes of the pieces. Beginning at the right of
the illustration: the skinny is ten times as large as
a bit, the flat is ten times as large as a skinny
(Question 2A–B), and the super bit is ten times as
large as a flat *(Question 2C).* Be sure students see

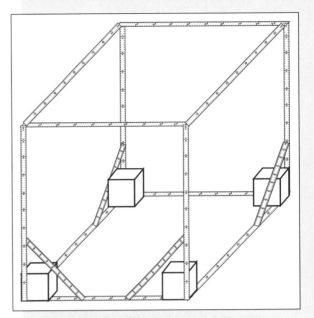

Figure 13: *A megabit constructed with 12 metersticks*

Content Note

The term "mega" often refers to 1,000,000. For example,
a megabyte of computer memory equals 1,000,000 bytes.

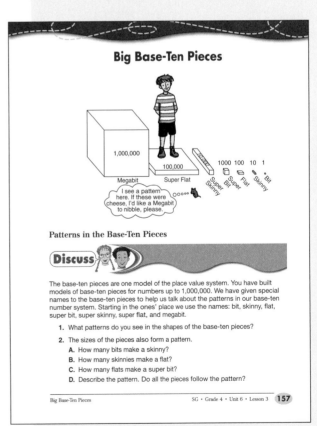

Student Guide - page 157 (Answers on p. 64)

We can write the value of each piece, using the powers of 10. For example, $100 = 10 \times 10$, and it can be written as 10^2. This is read as 10 to the second power or 10 squared. The number $1000 = 10 \times 10 \times 10$, and it can be written as 10^3. This is read as 10 to the third power. The following chart helps to show these patterns.

3. Draw the chart on your paper and fill in the missing spaces.

Base-Ten Chart

Base-Ten Piece	Written as a Power of 10	Value
Bit	1	1
Skinny	$1 \times 10 = 10^1$	
Flat		100
Super Bit	$10 \times 10 \times 10 = 10^3$	
Super Skinny		10,000
Super Flat		
Megabit		

Each repeating core pattern is called a period on the *Place Value Chart*. The bit-skinny-flat group makes up the **ones'** period. The super bit-super skinny-super flat group makes up the **thousands'** period. The megabit begins the **millions'** period.

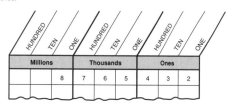

Millions			Thousands			Ones		
		8	7	6	5	4	3	2

Big Base-Ten Pieces

Student Guide - page 158 *(Answers on p. 64)*

Each period takes its name from the number that the cube represents in that period. In Lesson 1, you learned that a comma or space is placed between each period to make reading easier. Remember, the comma or space alerts you to say the period name. For instance: 8,765,432 is read as eight **million,** seven hundred sixty-five **thousand,** four hundred thirty-two.

Draw, Place, and Read

Play *Draw, Place, and Read*. Follow the directions that are written on the game page in the *Discovery Assignment Book*.

Tanya and Irma played *Draw, Place, and Read*. After all seven digit cards had been drawn, Tanya's number looked like this: 5,369,210. Irma's number looked like this: 6,935,021. Read each number.

4. Which girl recorded the larger number?

Homework

Play *Draw, Place, and Read* at home with your family.

Student Guide - page 159 *(Answers on p. 65)*

---

that this pattern continues with all the pieces. Each piece is ten times as large as the piece to its right *(Question 2D).*

Introduce the use of exponents to write the value of each base-ten piece. Explain that each column on the place value chart can be written as a power of 10. For example 10 is equal to 10^1, 100 is equal to 10×10 or 10^2, and 1000 is equal to $10 \times 10 \times 10$ or 10^3. Have students copy the chart in the *Student Guide* onto their own paper and use it to help them organize this information *(Question 3).* Students may question why 1 is not written as a power of 10. If this question comes up, ask the students what power of 10 might equal 1. It is possible that a student will continue the pattern in the exponents from the chart and suggest that this is 10^0. If this is suggested, you can add this to the Base-Ten Chart.

Connect the information in the Base-Ten Chart in *Question 3* with the information in *Place Value Chart II*. Discuss the division of the chart into periods. Each period is named after the cube or bit. We usually divide periods with a comma or a space when we write numbers.

Once students are comfortable with the *Place Value Chart II*, play the game *Draw, Place, and Read*. The directions are located in the *Discovery Assignment Book*. This can be played in small groups, as partners, or as a class.

Content Note

Numbers less than 10,000 are sometimes written without a comma to divide the ones' period from the thousands' period. For example, four thousand three hundred twenty-one can be written as 4,321 or 4321. *Math Trailblazers* does not include the comma in numbers that are less than 10,000.

Journal Prompt

Using the patterns in the *Place Value Chart II* and the shapes of the models that we built today, explain how you would construct a model for 10 million.

Math Facts

DPP items G, H, and J provide practice with the multiplication facts for the nines. Bit G is practice. Task H is skip counting on the calculator. Task J requires students to communicate their strategies in writing.

Homework and Practice

- Students take home the *Draw, Place, and Read* Game Page in the *Discovery Assignment Book* and play the game at home.

- DPP Bit I provides practice estimating with money.

- Home Practice Part 3 provides practice with paper-and-pencil computation and with estimation.

Answers for Part 3 of the Home Practice are in the Answer Key at the end of this lesson and at the end of this unit.

Assessment

Use the Journal Prompt to assess whether students see that each time you move to the left on the *Place Value Chart II* the number is ten times larger than the number to the immediate right and that the numbers increase by a power of ten. A model of ten million will be a megaskinny made up of ten megabits.

Name _____ Date _____

PART 3 **Addition and Subtraction Practice**

Use paper and pencil to solve the following problems. Use estimation to decide if your answers make sense. Explain your estimation strategy for F.

A. 4506
   + 8753

B. 5388
   + 9078

C. 9054
   − 2408

D. 7617
   − 4543

E. 3940
   + 6963

F. 10,415
   − 7593

PART 4 **Using Estimation**

The following table lists the number of people who immigrated to the United States from various countries in 2000. Use the information in the table to estimate the answers to the questions below. Use a separate sheet of paper to show what convenient numbers you chose to work with.

Country	Number of Immigrants	Country	Number of Immigrants
Canada	21,475	Mexico	171,748
China	41,861	Philippines	40,587
Dominican Republic	17,441	Romania	6,521
El Salvador	22,332	United Kingdom	14,532
India	39,072	Vietnam	25,340

1. Most immigrants came from which five countries listed in the table? List the countries and their number of immigrants. List the number of immigrants in order from largest to smallest.

2. About how many more people immigrated from Mexico than from China?

3. About how many people immigrated from Canada and Mexico combined?

4. The number of immigrants from El Salvador is about the same as the number from which other country?

5. About how many more people came from India than Romania?

6. In 2000, the number of immigrants from all countries totaled about 850,000 people. About how many immigrants are reported in the table above? (*Hint:* Use a calculator to help you with your estimation.)

68   DAB • Grade 4 • Unit 6   PLACE VALUE PATTERNS

Discovery Assignment Book - page 68 *(Answers on p. 65)*

Name _____ Date _____

Draw, Place, and Read

Players

This game can be played with 2 to 30 players. One player is the caller. If you have a large group, the game can be played with teams.

Materials

You will need 10 cards numbered 0–9.

Rules

Follow these directions:

1. Choose one person to be the caller. For each round, the caller will draw seven numbers. Decide ahead of time if the caller will replace each number after it has been recorded or if each number will be used only once in each round.

2. After each draw, players record the digit that was drawn in any column on the first row of the place value chart below. Once a digit has been recorded, it cannot be moved.

3. After all seven draws, the person who makes and reads the highest number earns a point. Move to the next row on the place value chart for the next round.

As an extra challenge, you can agree to use 8 or 9 draws instead of 7 for each round.

Millions' Period			Thousands' Period			Ones' Period		

Big Base-Ten Pieces   DAB • Grade 4 • Unit 6 • Lesson 3   **75**

Discovery Assignment Book - page 75

At a Glance

Math Facts and Daily Practice and Problems

DPP items G, H, and J provide practice with math facts. Bit I provides computation and estimation practice.

Part 1. Big Base-Ten Pieces

1. Students review the 10 for 1 relationship of the base-ten pieces using the *Place Value Chart II* Transparency Master.

2. In a teacher-guided activity, students extend the base-ten models to one million. Using the pattern established in base-ten blocks, students build a model for ten thousand, one hundred thousand, and one million. (To build a super skinny, students use two packs and four metersticks. A super skinny is the same as ten packs lined up in a row. A super flat is made with four packs and eight metersticks. It is the size and shape of 100 packs in ten rows of ten packs each. A megabit is made with four packs and 12 metersticks. It is the size and shape of 10 packs by 10 packs by 10 packs.)

3. Students look for patterns on the *Place Value Chart II* and in the base-ten pieces that represent the numbers in our base-ten system.

Part 2. Patterns in the Base-Ten Pieces

1. Read and discuss the *Big Base-Ten Pieces* Activity Pages in the *Student Guide*. *(Questions 1–2)*
2. Students write each place value up to 1,000,000 as a power of 10. *(Question 3)*
3. Play a round of the game *Draw, Place, and Read* using the game page in the *Discovery Assignment Book*.

Homework

1. Students play the game *Draw, Place, and Read* at home.
2. Assign Home Practice Part 3.

Assessment

Use the Journal Prompt as an assessment.

Answer Key is on pages 64–65.

Notes:

Digit Cards 0–9

4	9
3	8
2	7
1	6
0	5

Reverse Side of Digit Cards 0–9

Place Value Chart II

	Millions			Thousands			Ones	
HUNDRED	TEN	ONE	HUNDRED	TEN	ONE	HUNDRED	TEN	ONE

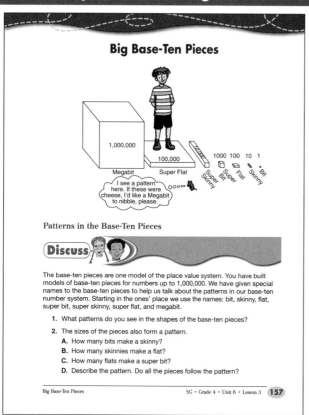

Student Guide - page 157

We can write the value of each piece, using the powers of 10. For example, $100 = 10 \times 10$, and it can be written as 10^2. This is read as 10 to the second power or 10 squared. The number $1000 = 10 \times 10 \times 10$, and it can be written as 10^3. This is read as 10 to the third power. The following chart helps to show these patterns.

3. Draw the chart on your paper and fill in the missing spaces.

Base-Ten Chart

Base-Ten Piece	Written as a Power of 10	Value
Bit	1	1
Skinny	$1 \times 10 = 10^1$	
Flat		100
Super Bit	$10 \times 10 \times 10 = 10^3$	
Super Skinny		10,000
Super Flat		
Megabit		

Each repeating core pattern is called a period on the *Place Value Chart.* The bit-skinny-flat group makes up the **ones'** period. The super bit-super skinny-super flat group makes up the **thousands'** period. The megabit begins the **millions'** period.

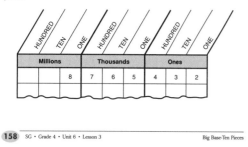

Big Base-Ten Pieces

Student Guide - page 158

Student Guide (p. 157)

Big Base-Ten Pieces

1. Beginning with the bit, the shapes form the pattern: bit (cube), skinny, flat, bit (cube), skinny, flat, bit (cube).*

2.* A. 10

   B. 10

   C. 10

   D. Each piece is 10 times as large as the piece to its right. All the pieces follow the pattern.

Student Guide (p. 158)

3.*

Base-Ten Chart

Base-Ten Piece	Written as a Power of 10	Value
Bit	1	1
Skinny	$1 \times 10 = 10^1$	10
Flat	$10 \times 10 = 10^2$	100
Super Bit	$10 \times 10 \times 10 = 10^3$	1,000
Super Skinny	$10 \times 10 \times 10 \times 10 = 10^4$	10,000
Super Flat	$10 \times 10 \times 10 \times 10 \times 10 = 10^5$	100,000
Megabit	$10 \times 10 \times 10 \times 10 \times 10 \times 10 = 10^6$	1,000,000

*Answers and/or discussion are included in the Lesson Guide.

Student Guide (p. 159)

4. Irma

Student Guide - page 159

Discovery Assignment Book (p. 68)

Home Practice*

Part 3. Addition and Subtraction Practice

A. 13,259

B. 14,446

C. 6646

D. 3074

E. 10,903

F. 2822; estimation strategies will vary.
Possible strategy: $10,500 - 7,500 = 3000$.

Name _____ Date _____

PART 3 Addition and Subtraction Practice

Use paper and pencil to solve the following problems. Use estimation to decide if your answers make sense. Explain your estimation strategy for F.

A.   4506
  + 8753

B.   5388
  + 9078

C.   9054
  − 2408

D.   7617
  − 4543

E.   3940
  + 6963

F.   10,415
  − 7593

PART 4 Using Estimation

The following table lists the number of people who immigrated to the United States from various countries in 2000. Use the information in the table to estimate the answers to the questions below. Use a separate sheet of paper to show what convenient numbers you chose to work with.

Country	Number of Immigrants	Country	Number of Immigrants
Canada	21,475	Mexico	171,748
China	41,861	Philippines	40,587
Dominican Republic	17,441	Romania	6,521
El Salvador	22,332	United Kingdom	14,532
India	39,072	Vietnam	25,340

1. Most immigrants came from which five countries listed in the table? List the countries and their number of immigrants. List the number of immigrants in order from largest to smallest.

2. About how many more people immigrated from Mexico than from China?

3. About how many people immigrated from Canada and Mexico combined?

4. The number of immigrants from El Salvador is about the same as the number from which other country?

5. About how many more people came from India than Romania?

6. In 2000, the number of immigrants from all countries totaled about 850,000 people. About how many immigrants are reported in the table above? (*Hint:* Use a calculator to help you with your estimation.)

68   DAB • Grade 4 • Unit 6   PLACE VALUE PATTERNS

Discovery Assignment Book - page 68

*Answers for all the Home Practice in the *Discovery Assignment Book* are at the end of the unit.

Lesson 4

News Number Line

Lesson Overview

Students create a number line from 1000 to 1,000,000 using a paper strip or string that is 10 meters long. Numbers are placed in order as in Lesson 1, but in this lesson placements also show the relative distances between the numbers. The activity helps students recognize relative sizes of the numbers through the millions.

Key Content

- Developing number sense for large numbers (to the millions).
- Using a number line to represent large numbers (from 1000 to 1 million).
- Using benchmark numbers to order large numbers (from 1000 to 1 million).

Key Vocabulary

- benchmarks
- million
- rounding

Math Facts

DPP items K and L provide practice with multiplication and division facts.

Homework

1. Assign the homework in the *Student Guide*. Omit **Questions 8–10** if Lesson 5 will be omitted.
2. Assign Part 6 of the Home Practice.

Assessment

1. Use homework **Questions 5–7** as a quiz.
2. Use the *Observational Assessment Record* to note students' abilities to order large numbers.

Materials List

Supplies and Copies

Student	Teacher
Supplies for Each Student Group	**Supplies**
• number newswire created in Lesson 1 • calculator	• 1 or 10 metersticks • red and green markers • 10-meter strip of adding machine tape, string, twine, or cord • paper clips
Copies	**Copies/Transparencies**

All blackline masters including assessment, transparency, and DPP masters are also on the Teacher Resource CD.

Student Books
News Number Line (*Student Guide* Pages 160–163)

Daily Practice and Problems and Home Practice
DPP items K–L (*Unit Resource Guide* Pages 21–22)
Home Practice Part 6 (*Discovery Assignment Book* Page 70)

Note: Classrooms whose pacing differs significantly from the suggested pacing of the units should use the Math Facts Calendar in Section 4 of the *Facts Resource Guide* to ensure students receive the complete math facts program.

Assessment Tools
Observational Assessment Record (*Unit Resource Guide* Pages 11–12)

K. Bit: Fact Families for × and ÷

(URG p. 21)

Complete the number sentences for the related facts.

A. $3 \times 9 =$ __

__ $\div 3 =$ __

__ $\div 9 =$ __

__ $\times 3 =$ __

B. $9 \times 7 =$ __

__ $\div 7 =$ __

__ $\div 9 =$ __

$7 \times$ __ $=$ __

C. $9 \times 9 =$ __

__ $\div 9 =$ __

D. $54 \div 9 =$ __

$9 \times$ __ $= 54$

$54 \div$ __ $= 9$

__ $\times 9 =$ __

E. $9 \times 4 =$ __

__ $\div 9 = 4$

__ $\div 4 =$ __

__ $\times 9 =$ __

L. Challenge: Who Am I? (URG p. 22)

1. I am a square number greater than 9. One of my two digits is 5 more than the other. Who am I?

2. I am a square number less than 100. One of my digits is 8 less than twice the other. Who am I?

3. Make up your own square number riddle and try it on a partner.

Before the Activity

To create the number line, we suggest using a 10-meter strip of adding machine tape. Creating the number line is described in Developing the Activity and shown in Figure 16. If adding machine tape is not available, here are two other options.

Option A

Use a 10-meter piece of string. Mark meters with a red marker and decimeters with a green marker. Each meter will represent 100,000 units on the number line. Each decimeter will represent 10,000 units. If your original newswire from Lesson 1 is 10 meters long, prepare it for this activity by sliding all the numbers to one end or removing them temporarily. Replace the numbers on the number line once the intervals have been marked. See Figure 17.

Option B

Cut 18 sheets of $8\frac{1}{2}$-by-11-inch paper in half lengthwise and tape these strips end to end to create a paper strip approximately 10 meters long. Mark meters and decimeters on the paper with red and green markers to represent intervals of 10,000 and 100,000.

Teaching the Activity

Ask students:

* *Count by 100,000s to 1 million. How many 100,000s are in a million?* (10).

Lay one meterstick along the top of the 10-meter strip of adding machine tape. Use a red marker to mark each end of the meterstick on the adding machine tape.

Label the left mark 0 and the right mark, 100,000. Explain to students that each meter will represent 100,000 units on this number line scale. See Figure 14. Ask:

* *How many metersticks will you need to mark off 1,000,000 units on the number line?* (10).

Lay 10 metersticks end-to-end along the adding machine tape. If your meterstick supply has been depleted by the model-constructing activity in Lesson 3, use one meterstick to mark off one-meter intervals. Use a red marker to record the numbers at the intervals (100,000, 200,000, 300,000, etc.) as students count, "one hundred thousand, two hundred thousand, three hundred thousand, . . . nine hundred thousand, and ten hundred thousand, or one million." Tell students they will use these numbers as guides, or **benchmarks,** to help them place numbers on the number line. Ask students:

* *What other benchmarks would be helpful in placing a number such as 37,000 on the number line?*
* *How can we divide each 100,000 to make it easier to place the numbers quickly on the number line?*

Guide students to see that the meter intervals can be subdivided into smaller units. Using metersticks, it is convenient to divide each 100,000 interval into 10 intervals of 10,000. Each decimeter (10 centimeters) will represent 10,000 units on the number line. Use a green marker to mark the intervals of 10,000 as students count, "zero, ten thousand, twenty thousand, thirty thousand, . . . ninety thousand, and one hundred thousand." Note that 100,000 is already marked. Ask students to finish marking the 10,000 intervals from 100,000 to 1 million. See Figure 15.

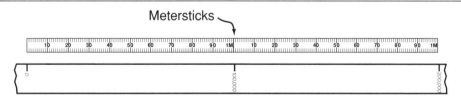

Figure 14: *Number line marked by hundred thousands*

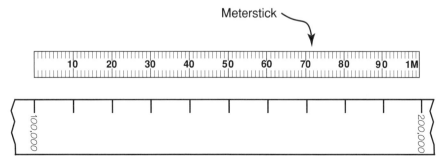

Figure 15: *Number line marked by ten thousands*

TIMS Tip

While some students finish marking the 10,000 intervals on the number line, have the rest of the class complete a DPP item.

If you use adding machine tape for your number line, the completed number line should look similar to the one in Figure 16. Use paper clips to attach each index card strip in the proper place along the number line.

If you use string for the number line, mark 100,000 and 10,000 intervals with red and green markers, respectively. Fold over a portion of the index card strip to form a small flap. Fold the flap over the string and use a paper clip to attach the card to the number line. This should keep the index cards from slipping. See Figure 17.

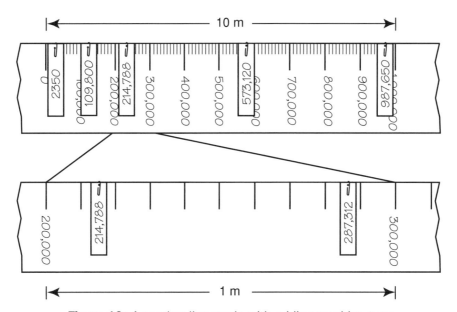

Figure 16: *A number line made with adding machine tape*

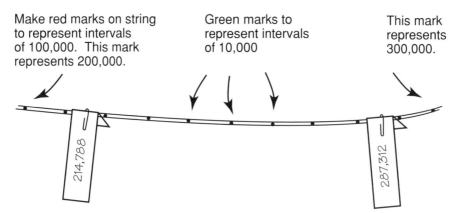

Figure 17: *A number line made with string*

When the number line is complete, model placing numbers on it.

1. Read the number.
2. Determine and state the 100,000 interval.
3. Determine the 10,000 interval. Name the two benchmarks you will use.
4. Explain why you are placing the number in that spot.

For example: *The number 214,788 should be placed in the interval between 200,000 and 300,000. Since 214 comes in the interval between 210 and 220, the number 214,788 should be placed in the interval between 210,000 and 220,000. I will place it close to the middle of the interval because 214,788 is about 215,000.* Repeat the modeling until students are comfortable with the sequence.

Ask student pairs to place one number from the newswire on the number line, following the same procedure. Use only numbers less than one million. If there is more time, have student pairs place a second number for additional practice.

Discuss extending the number line to place numbers greater than 1 million. To continue the proportional model, 10 metersticks would be needed to represent each million. Have students try to imagine where the number 18 million would be if the newswire number line were extended (18 × 10 meters = 180 meters). Ask:

- *Where would 18 million be?* (In the gym, in the parking lot, etc.) Discuss where small numbers, less than 1000, would be placed on this number line. Ask for examples of such numbers (e.g., number of students in the class, number of students in the school, the number of days in a year, etc.). These discussions will help students develop a clearer sense of the relative sizes of numbers.

Questions 1–3 on the *News Number Line* Activity Pages in the *Student Guide* provide more opportunities to work with 1 million. *Questions 1–2* ask students to skip count by 100,000s and 10,000s to 1 million using a calculator. See the TIMS Tip on this page.

TIMS Tip

Pressing  on many four-function calculators will continuously add 10,000. You may need to test the calculators used in your classroom before presenting this to students. If it does not work, consult the manual that came with your particular model of calculator to find the correct sequence of keystrokes.

News Number Line

How Big Is One Million?

1. Use your calculator to count by 10,000s to 1 million. If you count out loud, how many numbers will you say? Begin this way, "ten thousand, twenty thousand, thirty thousand, . . ."

2. Use your calculator to count by 100,000s to 1 million. If you count out loud, how many numbers will you say? Begin this way, "one hundred thousand, two hundred thousand, three hundred thousand, . . ."

3. A pencil manufacturer donates 1,000,000 pencils to your school. Your principal divides the pencils evenly among the students. How many pencils will each student get?
   A. What do you need to know before you can solve the problem?
   B. Use your calculator to find the answer.

Student Guide - page 160 (Answers on p. 75)

Questions 3 asks students to use a calculator to find the number of pencils each student would get if they divided 1 million pencils equally among all the students in the school. They will need to know the number of students in the school to answer the question.

In Unit 4, students used their calculators to determine if a number is a factor of another number by checking to see if it would divide evenly into the number, that is, if the answer is a whole number. Depending on the number of students in your school, a million pencils may not be divided evenly. In interpreting their answers, remind students that numbers to the right of the decimal point mean that the number will not come out evenly and there will be some pencils left over.

Math Facts

DPP Bit K provides practice with the multiplication and division facts for the nines through the use of fact families. Challenge L is a riddle using the square numbers.

Homework and Practice

- *Questions 1–7* in the Homework section in the *Student Guide* provide practice ordering large numbers and writing them in words.

- Assign *Questions 8–10* in the Homework section only if you plan to complete Lesson 5. These questions ask students to bring in jars filled with objects to be used in Lesson 5.

- Part 6 of the Home Practice helps build mental math skills through extensions of subtraction facts strategies.

Answers for Part 6 of the Home Practice are in the Answer Key at the end of this lesson and at the end of this unit.

Assessment

- Use homework *Questions 5–7* as a quiz.
- Use the *Observational Assessment Record* to record students' abilities to order large numbers using one thousand, ten thousand, hundred thousand, and one million as benchmarks.

Taking Attendance

Museum Attendance in 2001 and 2002

Museum	Attendance in 2001 and 2002	
	2001	2002
Science Museum	1,890,227	1,985,609
Institute of Art	1,338,266	1,295,321
Children's Museum	1,295,755	1,227,062
Aquarium and Oceanarium	1,858,766	1,789,222
Museum of the Stars	577,997	458,156

1. Put the 2001 attendance numbers in order from smallest to largest.

2. Name the most popular museum in 2001.

3. Which museum's attendance was closest to 1,000,000 in 2001?

4. Which museum had fewer visitors in 2001 than it had in 2002?

5. Put the 2002 attendance numbers in order from smallest to largest.

6. Name the least popular museum in 2002.

7. Write the 2002 attendance for each museum in words.

Student Guide - page 161 (Answers on p. 75)

Making Mystery Jars

The next three problems prepare for the next lesson, *Close Enough*. If your class is not going to do Lesson 5, you may skip these questions.

8. Here is a picture Linda made using a computer.

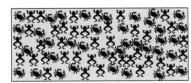

There are about 15 animals in the small picture at the right. Use this number as a reference number to help you estimate the number of animals in the picture above.

In the next lesson, you will use the same idea you used in Question 8 to estimate the number of objects in jars.

9. Bring in a mystery jar of objects to use in the activity.

- Find a clear, clean jar with a lid.
- Fill (or partly fill) the jar with one kind of object such as beans, pasta, or small building blocks. The objects should be small and about the same size.
- Count the objects in your jar. Write the number of objects on a small piece of paper. Tape the paper to the inside of the lid. Put the lid on the jar so that no one can see the number.
- Put your name on the outside of the lid.

Student Guide - page 162 (Answers on p. 76)

One way to make good estimates is to compare the mystery jar to another jar or bag with a known number of objects. The picture below shows Ana's mystery jar of marbles and a bag with 50 marbles. Other students can use the 50 marbles as a reference to estimate the number of marbles in the mystery jar.

10. Bring in a number of objects in another jar or in a plastic bag. Your classmates will use this number as a reference to help them estimate the number of objects in your mystery jar.

- Use the same objects that are in your mystery jar. Count out a convenient number of objects—10, 25, 50, or 100 objects work well.
- Place them in another jar or a clear plastic bag.
- Label the jar (or bag) with your name and the number of objects so your classmates can see this number.

Student Guide - page 163

Name _____ Date _____

PART 6   Subtraction Count Backs

Do these problems in your head. Write only the answers. Work across the rows.

A. 11 – 2 = _____   B. 31 – 2 = _____

C. 110 – 20 = _____   D. 310 – 20 = _____

E. 27 – 3 = _____   F. 7 – 3 = _____

G. 2700 – 300 _____   H. 70 – 30 = _____

I. 12 – 3 = _____   J. 52 – 3 = _____

K. 120 – 30 = _____   L. 5200 – 300 = _____

Describe any patterns you see.

PART 7   Convenient Numbers

Estimate where each of the numbers (A–D) is located on the following number line. Make a mark on the number line to show each number. Label each mark with the correct letter A, B, C, or D. Then use the number line to round each number to the nearest ten thousand and nearest hundred thousand.

```
◄────┼─────┼─────┼─────┼─────┼────►
  500,000 600,000 700,000 800,000 900,000
```

	Nearest ten thousand	Nearest hundred thousand
A. 650,780	_____	_____
B. 870,002	_____	_____
C. 720,000	_____	_____
D. 509,237	_____	_____

Discovery Assignment Book - page 70 (Answers on p. 76)

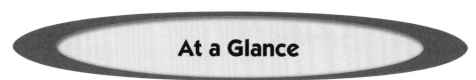
Math Facts and Daily Practice and Problems

DPP items K and L provide practice with multiplication and division facts.

Teaching the Activity

1. Students construct a number line from 1000 to 1,000,000 with intervals marked at each 10,000 and 100,000.
2. Students place the numbers from the newswire created in Lesson 1 on the number line.
3. Students read and discuss questions on the *News Number Line* Activity Pages in the *Student Guide*.

Homework

1. Assign the homework in the *Student Guide*. Omit **Questions 8–10** if Lesson 5 will be omitted.
2. Assign Part 6 of the Home Practice.

Assessment

1. Use homework **Questions 5–7** as a quiz.
2. Use the *Observational Assessment Record* to note students' abilities to order large numbers.

Answer Key is on pages 75–76.

Notes:

Student Guide (p. 160)

News Number Line

1. 100 numbers

2. 10 numbers

3. A.–B. Answers will vary. You need to know how many students are in the school.

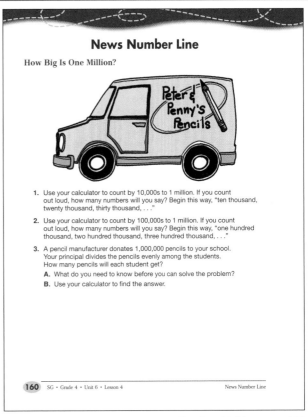

News Number Line

How Big Is One Million?

1. Use your calculator to count by 10,000s to 1 million. If you count out loud, how many numbers will you say? Begin this way, "ten thousand, twenty thousand, thirty thousand, . . ."

2. Use your calculator to count by 100,000s to 1 million. If you count out loud, how many numbers will you say? Begin this way, "one hundred thousand, two hundred thousand, three hundred thousand, . . ."

3. A pencil manufacturer donates 1,000,000 pencils to your school. Your principal divides the pencils evenly among the students. How many pencils will each student get?

   A. What do you need to know before you can solve the problem?

   B. Use your calculator to find the answer.

160   SG • Grade 4 • Unit 6 • Lesson 4   News Number Line

Student Guide - page 160

Student Guide (p. 161)

Homework

1. 577,997; 1,295,755; 1,338,266; 1,858,766; 1,890,227

2. Science Museum

3. Children's Museum

4. Science Museum

5. 458,156; 1,227,062; 1,295,321; 1,789,222; 1,985,609

6. Museum of the Stars

7. one million, nine hundred eighty-five thousand, six hundred nine; one million, two hundred ninety-five thousand, three hundred twenty-one; one million, two hundred twenty-seven thousand, sixty-two; one million, seven hundred eighty-nine thousand, two hundred twenty-two; four hundred fifty-eight thousand, one hundred fifty-six

Homework

Taking Attendance

Museum Attendance in 2001 and 2002

Museum	Attendance in 2001 and 2002	
	2001	2002
Science Museum	1,890,227	1,985,609
Institute of Art	1,338,266	1,295,321
Children's Museum	1,295,755	1,227,062
Aquarium and Oceanarium	1,858,766	1,789,222
Museum of the Stars	577,997	458,156

1. Put the 2001 attendance numbers in order from smallest to largest.

2. Name the most popular museum in 2001.

3. Which museum's attendance was closest to 1,000,000 in 2001?

4. Which museum had fewer visitors in 2001 than it had in 2002?

5. Put the 2002 attendance numbers in order from smallest to largest.

6. Name the least popular museum in 2002.

7. Write the 2002 attendance for each museum in words.

News Number Line   SG • Grade 4 • Unit 6 • Lesson 4   161

Student Guide - page 161

Student Guide (p. 162)

8. Estimates will vary. Accept estimates between 70–80 animals.

Making Mystery Jars

The next three problems prepare for the next lesson, *Close Enough*. If your class is not going to do Lesson 5, you may skip these questions.

8. Here is a picture Linda made using a computer.

There are about 15 animals in the small picture at the right. Use this number as a reference number to help you estimate the number of animals in the picture above.

In the next lesson, you will use the same idea you used in Question 8 to estimate the number of objects in jars.

9. Bring in a mystery jar of objects to use in the activity.
- Find a clear, clean jar with a lid.
- Fill (or partly fill) the jar with one kind of object such as beans, pasta, or small building blocks. The objects should be small and about the same size.
- Count the objects in your jar. Write the number of objects on a small piece of paper. Tape the paper to the inside of the lid. Put the lid on the jar so that no one can see the number.
- Put your name on the outside of the lid.

162 SG • Grade 4 • Unit 6 • Lesson 4   News Number Line

Student Guide - page 162

Discovery Assignment Book (p. 70)

Home Practice*

Part 6. Subtraction Count Backs

A. 9

B. 29

C. 90

D. 290

E. 24

F. 4

G. 2400

H. 40

I. 9

J. 49

K. 90

L. 4900

Descriptions of patterns will vary.

Name _____ Date _____

PART 6 Subtraction Count Backs

Do these problems in your head. Write only the answers. Work across the rows.

A. $11 - 2 =$ _____   B. $31 - 2 =$ _____

C. $110 - 20 =$ _____   D. $310 - 20 =$ _____

E. $27 - 3 =$ _____   F. $7 - 3 =$ _____

G. $2700 - 300 =$ _____   H. $70 - 30 =$ _____

I. $12 - 3 =$ _____   J. $52 - 3 =$ _____

K. $120 - 30 =$ _____   L. $5200 - 300 =$ _____

Describe any patterns you see.

PART 7 Convenient Numbers

Estimate where each of the numbers (A–D) is located on the following number line. Make a mark on the number line to show each number. Label each mark with the correct letter A, B, C, or D. Then use the number line to round each number to the nearest ten thousand and nearest hundred thousand.

500,000   600,000   700,000   800,000   900,000

	Nearest ten thousand	Nearest hundred thousand
A. 650,780	_____	_____
B. 870,002	_____	_____
C. 720,000	_____	_____
D. 509,237	_____	_____

Copyright © Kendall/Hunt Publishing Company

70 DAB • Grade 4 • Unit 6   PLACE VALUE PATTERNS

Discovery Assignment Book - page 70

*Answers for all the Home Practice in the *Discovery Assignment Book* are at the end of the unit.

Close Enough

Lesson Overview

Estimated Class Sessions
2-3

This lesson has two parts. In Part 1, students bring in jars filled with small objects as part of the homework assignment from the previous lesson. In class they estimate the number of objects in the jars by comparing the objects in the jars with a known number of objects. They record their estimates in a table. Through a teacher-led discussion, the class decides which estimates are close to the actual number by counting the objects and deciding which estimates are within 10% of the actual number. They learn methods for approximating 10% of a number using counters and calculators.

In Part 2 of the lesson, students answer questions in the *Student Guide*. They discuss the idea that deciding an estimate is close to the actual number depends on the size of the number.

Key Content

- Estimating the number of objects in a collection.
- Estimating 10% of a number.
- Using 10% as a standard for error analysis.

Key Vocabulary

- estimate
- within 10%

Homework

Assign the Homework section in the *Student Guide*.

Assessment

Use *Questions 1–2* in the Homework section as an assessment.

Curriculum Sequence

Before This Unit

How Close Are Estimates?

In previous units, students have made predictions and estimates as part of activities and experiments. For example, in the *Bouncing Ball* lab in Unit 5, students predicted the bounce height of a ball, then checked the prediction to see if the actual bounce height was close to the predicted bounce height. They used a standard set by the teacher or the class to decide if their predictions were close enough.

Percents

Students were introduced to percents in Grade 3 Unit 14 Lesson 3 *Tracking Our Reading.* They used 25%, 50%, 75%, and 100% as goals in a reading survey.

After This Unit

How Close Are Estimates?

For the remainder of the year, students can use 10% as a standard for deciding if predictions and estimates are close. See the *Volume vs. Number* lab in Unit 8 Lesson 3 for an example.

Materials List

Supplies and Copies

Student	Teacher
Supplies for Each Student • calculator • mystery jar from Lesson 4 homework	**Supplies** • meterstick • clear centimeter ruler • clear jar filled with 123 objects, optional • large and small clear jars, optional • objects for estimation such as connecting cubes, marbles, or beans, optional
Copies • 1 copy of *Three-column Data Table* per student group, optional (*Unit Resource Guide* Page 47)	**Copies/Transparencies** • 1 transparency of *10% Chart* or large paper for class data table (*Discovery Assignment Book* Page 77) • 1 transparency of *Three-column Data Table,* optional (*Unit Resource Guide* Page 47)

All blackline masters including assessment, transparency, and DPP masters are also on the Teacher Resource CD.

Student Books

Making Mystery Jars section from Lesson 4 (*Student Guide* Pages 162–163)
Close Enough (*Student Guide* Pages 164–168)
10% Chart (*Discovery Assignment Book* Page 77)

Making Mystery Jars

The next three problems prepare for the next lesson, *Close Enough.* If your class is not going to do Lesson 5, you may skip these questions.

8. Here is a picture Linda made using a computer.

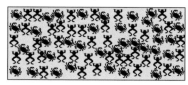

There are about 15 animals in the small picture at the right. Use this number as a reference number to help you estimate the number of animals in the picture above.

In the next lesson, you will use the same idea you used in Question 8 to estimate the number of objects in jars.

9. Bring in a mystery jar of objects to use in the activity.
   - Find a clear, clean jar with a lid.
   - Fill (or partly fill) the jar with one kind of object such as beans, pasta, or small building blocks. The objects should be small and about the same size.
   - Count the objects in your jar. Write the number of objects on a small piece of paper. Tape the paper to the inside of the lid. Put the lid on the jar so that no one can see the number.
   - Put your name on the outside of the lid.

Student Guide - page 162

One way to make good estimates is to compare the mystery jar to another jar or bag with a known number of objects. The picture below shows Ana's mystery jar of marbles and a bag with 50 marbles. Other students can use the 50 marbles as a reference to estimate the number of marbles in the mystery jar.

10. Bring in a number of objects in another jar or in a plastic bag. Your classmates will use this number as a reference to help them estimate the number of objects in your mystery jar.
   - Use the same objects that are in your mystery jar. Count out a convenient number of objects—10, 25, 50, or 100 objects work well.
   - Place them in another jar or a clear plastic bag.
   - Label the jar (or bag) with your name and the number of objects so your classmates can see this number.

Student Guide - page 163

Before the Activity

Students complete Making Mystery Jars, ***Questions 8–10*** of the Homework section of the previous lesson *News Number Line.* They bring in jars of objects for classmates to estimate along with a convenient number (e.g., 10, 25, 50, or 100) of the same objects. These are counted and labeled to aid in the estimating. Select and display an assortment of about half the mystery jars to use in the first part of the lesson. You will need jars with a small number of objects and jars with a large number of objects. Save some jars for more practice in the second part of the lesson and to use as DPP items in later lessons and units.

Students will learn to find 10% of a number using the numbers of objects in the mystery jars as examples. The discussion prompts use a jar with 123 objects as an example. If you wish to follow the prompts exactly as written, include a jar with 123 objects such as marbles or centimeter connecting cubes with students' jars. Put 50 of the same object in another jar for students to use as a reference number when they estimate.

TIMS Tip

Since the lesson involves comparing large and small estimates, prepare one large and one small mystery jar to use in the discussion in case students do not bring in appropriate jars. A quart jar of marbles or connecting cubes and a baby food jar of the same object work well. Count out an additional number of objects (50 or 100) to show students so they can make informed estimates. They can compare the known number of objects to the objects in the mystery jar.

Teaching the Activity

Part 1 Estimating the Number of Objects in Mystery Jars

To begin the activity, discuss ***Question 8*** from the Homework section in the *Student Guide* of the previous lesson. Students must estimate the number of animals in a larger picture when given the number of animals in a smaller picture. Discuss students' estimation strategies. Highlight strategies that include estimating the number of times the small picture will fit into the larger picture (about 5), then multiplying this estimate by the number of animals in the smaller picture (15). Since $5 \times 15 = 75$, 75 animals is a good estimate. Point out that a similar method is used to estimate the size of a crowd at concerts, sports events, and political rallies.

To help students think through the estimation process, choose a student's mystery jar and ask them to estimate the number of objects in it.

Show the class the reference number of objects the student brought with the mystery jar. For example, if the student brought 100 objects as a reference, say:

- *Here are 100 objects. Estimate the number of objects in the mystery jar.*
- *Do you think there are more than 10 or less than 10?*
- *Do you think there are more than 100 objects in the jar or less than 100?*
- *Do you think there are more than 500 or less than 500?*

Discuss possible estimation strategies, then tell students they will estimate the number of objects in each mystery jar you selected for this part of the lesson. First, direct students to begin a data table as shown in Figure 18. (Students may use a copy of a *Three-column Data Table* or make their own.)

Place the mystery jars at various stations throughout the room. Allow students to circulate throughout the room and make their estimates. They should fill in their data tables with the names on each jar, the type of object, and their estimate.

When students finish making their estimates, open the lids and tell the exact number of objects in each jar. The following discussion prompts use the estimates in the data table in Figure 18 as examples. Use the prompts to help guide a discussion on what it means to be close. (See the TIMS Tutor: *Estimation, Accuracy, and Error* for a more detailed discussion on making estimates and deciding if estimates are close enough.) Open one of the larger jars and tell the class the actual number of objects in the jar. Ask:

- *Whose estimates match the actual number exactly?* (Chances are good that very few, if any, of the students will be able to guess the exact number of objects.)
- *Whose estimates are close?* (More students will be able to say that their estimates are close.)
- *Which estimates are close enough to the actual number to be good estimates? How much larger or smaller can your estimate be and still be a good estimate?* (Let students choose a range of values that makes sense to them. They may say that the estimates must be within 10 or 20 objects to be close. Any reasonable range will do for now. For example, if the actual number of beans in Michael's jar is 286 beans, then students may choose to accept estimates within 10 or 20 beans of 286.)

Mystery Jar Estimates		
Name on Jar	**Object**	**Estimate**
Teacher's Name	cubes	140
Michael	beans	275
Irma	pasta shells	20

Figure 18: *Sample student data table of estimates of mystery jars*

Choose one of the smaller jars and tell the class the actual number of objects in the jar. Ask:

- *Whose estimates match the actual number exactly?*
- *Whose estimates are close?*
- *Which estimates are close enough to the actual number to be good estimates? How much larger or smaller can your estimate be and still be a good estimate?* (At first, students may choose the same range of values as they did for the larger jar. For example, if there are actually 25 pasta shells in Irma's jar, students may say that good estimates may also be within 10 of the exact number. However, other students may say that estimates as low as 15 and as high as 35 pasta shells are not good estimates.)
- *Do you think it is fair to judge our estimates for both the large and small jars using the same range (a range of 10 or 20 objects)?* (Students should begin to see that the larger the number of objects, the larger the range of acceptable values and the smaller the number of objects, the smaller the range of acceptable values. It is clear that we cannot use a difference of 20 objects as our standard for both Michael's and Irma's jars. Estimates within 20 beans of 286 beans, such as 305 beans, can be considered good estimates. Using the same range, however, for the number of pasta shells in Irma's jar is not appropriate. Estimates as low as 5 and as high as 45 shells should not be considered good estimates when the actual number is 25 shells.)
- *If there are 474 students in the school, is an estimate of 500 students close enough?* (In many situations, yes.)
- *If there are 27 students in the classroom, is an estimate of 1 student close enough?* (Obviously, no.)

At this point in the lesson, tell students that the class is going to consider appropriate standards for deciding if estimates and predictions are close. We want a standard that gives us a larger range for big numbers than for small numbers. One way to do this is to use percent. For example, we could decide that "close enough" means "within 10%." That is, an estimate is close enough if it is within 10% of the actual number. Ten percent means 10 out of every 100 or 1 out of every 10. Therefore, for every 10 marbles in a jar, an estimate can be off by 1 marble.

Use the following prompts to discuss 10% of a number. You can choose one student's jar as an example and adapt the prompts based on the number of objects in the jar. Or, use a jar with 123 objects as your example (as described in Before the Activity). Students will need calculators.

Content Note

Why 10%? Using 10% as a benchmark is not always appropriate. If carpenters made errors as large as 10% of their specifications when making doors, many doors would not close. However, for classroom purposes 10% is a good standard for the following reasons:

1. It's easy to find 10%, or at least to estimate it.
2. In many of the hands-on experiments students do, 10% is about the level of accuracy we can expect from students using the equipment they have, while 10% accuracy is still good enough for seeing the patterns in data on graphs.
3. Psychologically, 10% is near the limit of our visual estimating ability. For example, if you show a person two drawings in sequence, one an enlargement of the other, in most cases that person will have difficulty telling which one is 10% larger.

- *There are exactly 123 connecting cubes in my jar. 100% means one whole or all the connecting cubes. How many connecting cubes is 100% of the cubes?* (123)

- *50% means 50 out of 100 or $\frac{1}{2}$. About how many cubes are 50% of the cubes?* (About 60 cubes.)

- *10% means 10 out of every 100 or $\frac{1}{10}$. One way to find 10% or $\frac{1}{10}$ of the cubes is to divide them into 10 groups. Use the cubes from the jar to divide the 123 cubes into 10 equal groups. How many cubes are in each group? What is $\frac{1}{10}$ or 10% of 123?* (Since there are 10 groups of 12 cubes with 3 cubes left over, 10% is about 12 cubes.)

- *What operation did we use to divide the cubes into 10 groups, addition, subtraction, multiplication, or division?* (Division)

- *We can use division to find 10% of a number or $\frac{1}{10}$ of a number. Use your calculator to divide 123 by 10. What shows on your display?* (12.3)

- *10% of 123 is about what number?* (12. To show students that 12.3 is close to 12, use a centimeter ruler as a number line. Locate 12.3 cm on a centimeter ruler and ask students to find the closest whole centimeter.)

- *How low can your estimate be and still be within 10% of the actual number of 123 cubes?* (123 − 12 = 111 cubes)

- *How high can your estimate be and still be within 10% of the actual number?* (123 + 12 = 135 cubes)

- *So, what is the range of numbers that are within 10% of 123?* (111 cubes to 135 cubes)

- *Look at your data tables. My jar has exactly 123 cubes. Whose estimates are within 10%?*

Make a class data table using a transparency of the *10% Chart* in the *Discovery Assignment Book* or use the same headings on easel paper as shown in Figure 20. Tell students to use their copy of the *10% Chart* and fill in the first row with the appropriate information for the mystery jar you used. The data for the jar with 123 cubes is used as an example.

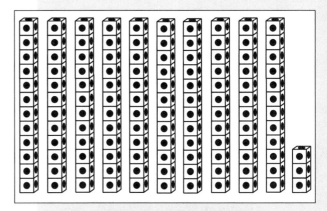

Figure 19: *To find 10% of 123 cubes, divide the cubes into 10 equal groups*

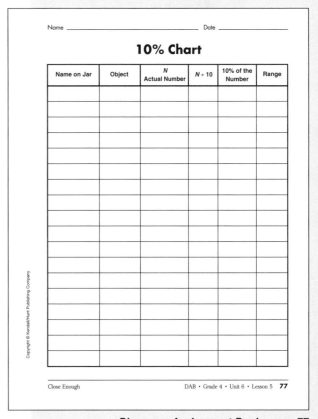

Discovery Assignment Book - page 77

10% Chart

Name on Jar	Object	N Actual Number	N ÷ 10	10% of the Number	Range
Teacher's Name	cubes	123	12.3	About 12	111–135
Michael	beans	286	28.6	About 28 or 29	258–314
Irma	pasta shells	25	2.5	2 or 3	22–28

Figure 20: *Sample 10% Chart*

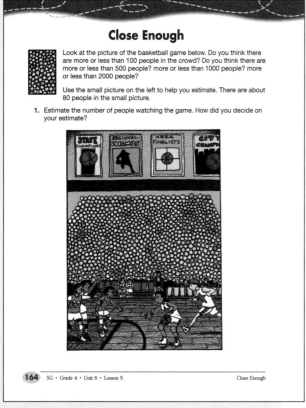

Close Enough

Look at the picture of the basketball game below. Do you think there are more or less than 100 people in the crowd? Do you think there are more or less than 500 people? more or less than 1000 people? more or less than 2000 people?

Use the small picture on the left to help you estimate. There are about 80 people in the small picture.

1. Estimate the number of people watching the game. How did you decide on your estimate?

164   SG • Grade 4 • Unit 6 • Lesson 5   Close Enough

Student Guide - page 164 *(Answers on p. 88)*

Students in Mrs. Dewey's room made mystery jars for homework and brought them to class. Three jars the students
Mrs. De
connect

Linda and Romesh estimated the number of objects in each jar and recorded their estimates in data tables. Here are their estimates:

Linda's Data Table

Object	Estimate
marbles	130
marshmallows	50
beans	350
cubes	500

Romesh's Data Table

Object	Estimate
marbles	120
marshmallows	35
beans	375
cubes	600

 Discuss

2. The actual number of marbles is 142. The actual number of marshmallows is 38.

   A. What is the difference between Linda's estimate of the number of marbles and the actual number?

Close Enough   SG • Grade 4 • Unit 6 • Lesson 5   165

Student Guide - page 165 *(Answers on p. 88)*

Choose another mystery jar and calculate 10% of the actual number of objects by using manipulatives or calculators. Fill in the data table with the appropriate information. Since we only need an approximation of 10%, we can round or truncate the values in the fourth column ($N \div 10$) to find the values in the fifth column (10% of the Number).

Continue filling in the *10% Chart* as a whole class. Students can work with you and fill in their own copy of the *10% Chart.* Or give students the actual number of objects in each remaining mystery jar by filling in the first two columns on the chart. Ask groups to complete several rows and report their results to the whole class.

As you fill in the table, ask students to look for patterns. They should see that dividing a number by 10 results in moving the decimal point one place to the left. To approximate 10% of a number, they can round or truncate this quotient. Students should see that they can get a pretty good estimate for 10% of a whole number by dropping the ones' digit.

- *What happens to the range of acceptable estimates as the numbers get larger?* (The range gets larger.)
- *What happens to the range when the actual numbers get smaller?* (The range gets smaller.)

Part 2 When Are Estimates Close Enough?

After students have completed the table, they are ready to discuss the questions in the *Student Guide.*

Question 1 asks students to estimate the number of people in the crowd watching the basketball game pictured on the first page of the *Close Enough* Activity Pages. Encourage them to use the number of people in the small picture as a reference number. As students report their estimates to the class, encourage them to explain their estimation strategies. How can we know if our estimate is close enough? In this case we may have to be satisfied with knowing that we have used good strategies to make the estimates since it would be difficult to count each person. There are approximately 900 people in the picture.

Question 2 reviews the notion of relative error: If the actual number of marbles in a jar is 142, then 130 is a pretty good estimate. But, if the actual number of marshmallows in a baby food jar is 38, 50 is not as good an estimate. Although in both cases the difference between the actual number and the estimate is 12, the error should be smaller when the number of objects is smaller. For example, if the actual number of marbles in a film canister is 12, then 24 is not a good estimate. Again the difference between the actual number and the estimate is 12, but the estimate is off by 100%.

Following these first two questions, the text and questions review the use of 10% as a guideline for deciding which estimates are close enough. Ten percent is defined as one-tenth of a number. Two methods for finding 10% of a number are discussed: using manipulatives to find one-tenth and using a calculator to divide by 10. Students may also use the pattern they found in Part 1.

Using the example of an actual number of 142 marbles in a jar, *Question 3* asks for estimates which are within 10% of 142. Since Linda's estimate of 130 marbles is between 128 and 156, her estimate is within 10%. However, Romesh's estimate of 120 marbles lies outside the range, so his estimate is not within 10%.

Question 4 repeats the process using the number of marshmallows in the baby food jar. Students can first find 10% of 38. If they use a calculator to divide 38 by 10, the display will show 3.8. With some discussion they see that 3.8 is between three and four, and closer to four. Students may be more comfortable with truncating than rounding, so they may use three marshmallows to calculate the range of acceptable values. Although allowing estimates within three marshmallows of 38 narrows the range, all the values within this range will still be within 10%. Romesh made an estimate for the number of marshmallows in the baby food jar which is within 10% of 38, but Linda did not.

Questions 5–7 provide more practice finding 10% of a number and identifying estimates that are within 10%. For more practice, have the class repeat the estimation process using different mystery jars. Be sure to add these numbers to the class *10% Chart* and continue to analyze the pattern in the chart.

Question 8 asks students to apply the procedure to a measurement situation, and *Question 9* asks students about a situation in which an error of 10% would not be acceptable.

Journal Prompt

How can you find 10% of a number? Describe all the ways you know.

B. What is the difference between Linda's estimate of the number of marshmallows and the actual number?

C. Is Linda's estimate for the number of marbles better than her estimate for the number of marshmallows? Why, or why not?

 Mrs. Dewey said: "Let's say that an estimate is 'close enough' if it is within ten percent. Ten percent (10%) means 10 out of every 100. That's the same as 1 out of every 10 or $\frac{1}{10}$. So, to find out which numbers are within 10% of 142, we have to find $\frac{1}{10}$ of 142. How can we do that?"

Linda chose to find $\frac{1}{10}$ of 142 by dividing the marbles into 10 equal groups. When she finished, each group had 14 marbles, and two marbles were left over. She decided that $\frac{1}{10}$ of 142 is about 14.

Romesh used a calculator to find $\frac{1}{10}$ of 142. He divided 142 by 10. Since the display read 14.2, he agreed with Linda: 10% of 142 is about 14.

Any prediction in the range between 128 and 156 is within 10% of 142, since:

$$142 - 14 = 128$$
and
$$142 + 14 = 156.$$

3. A. Look back at Linda's and Romesh's estimates listed in the data tables. Which of the estimates for the jar of marbles is within 10% of 142?

B. Do you agree that this estimate is close enough?

4. A. Find 10% of 38. Check your answer by finding 10% of 38 in a different way.

B. Look back at Linda's and Romesh's estimates listed in the data tables. Which of the estimates for the jar of marshmallows is within 10%?

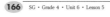

Student Guide - page 166 (Answers on p. 89)

---

5. Draw the following data table on your paper. Complete the table.

Object	N Actual Number	N ÷ 10	10% of the Number	Range
marbles	142	14.2	About 14	128–156
marshmallows	38			
beans	351			
cubes	526			

6. A. Is Linda's estimate for the number of beans within 10%? Why or why not?

B. Is the estimate Romesh made for the number of beans within 10%? Why or why not?

7. A. Is Linda's estimate for the number of cubes within 10%? Why or why not?

B. Is the estimate Romesh made for the number of cubes within 10%? Why or why not?

8. Estimate the height of the door to your classroom to the nearest cm.

A. Record your estimate and share it with your class.

B. Measure the height of the door to the nearest cm.

C. Which estimates are within 10% of the actual measurement?

9. A carpenter is making a door. The opening is 75 cm wide. If the carpenter measures the width of the door to within 10%, will the measurement be close enough? Why or why not?

Homework

Dear Family Member:

The students have learned to find 10% of various objects by finding one-tenth of the number. They can divide the number of objects into ten equal groups and count the number of objects in one group, or they can use a calculator to divide the number by ten. Ask your child to describe how he or she finds 10% of a number.

Thank you.

Student Guide - page 167 (Answers on p. 89)

Assign the Homework section in the *Student Guide.*

Use *Questions 1–2* in the Homework section as a short assessment.

A bar graph similar to the one in Figure 21 can help students identify the estimates that are within 10% of a number. Students can build a class graph by writing their estimates on an adhesive-backed piece of paper and placing it on the appropriate bar.

Students can use books such as those in the *Great Waldo Search* series to practice estimation. Ask students to estimate the number of objects on a given page. To help with their estimations, they can use an index card or small paper rectangle as a template. First, they count the number of objects covered by the template. Then, to obtain an estimate, they can multiply the number of objects covered by the template by the number of times the template will fit on the page.

---

1. Here is part of the *10% Chart* made by students in Mrs. Dewey's class. Complete the table.

Object	N Actual Number	N ÷ 10	10% of the Number	Range
blocks	51			
macaroni	632			
pennies	198			
Super Balls	15			

2. A. Is an estimate of 60 blocks within 10% of the actual number? Show how you know.

B. Is an estimate of 650 macaroni pieces within 10% of the actual number? Show how you know.

C. Is an estimate of 175 pennies within 10% of the actual number? Show how you know.

D. Is an estimate of 18 Super Balls within 10% of the actual number? Show how you know.

3. Tanya is working on the *Bouncing Ball* experiment. She predicts that the tennis ball will bounce to a height of 50 cm if it is dropped from a height of 100 cm. She checks her prediction, and the ball actually bounces to a height of 54 cm. Is her prediction of 50 cm within 10% of the actual bounce height of 54 cm? Why, or why not?

4. The average height of students in Room 204 is 55 inches. Nila is 48 inches tall. Is her height within 10% of the average height?

5. Keenya goes to the store with $32 for groceries. As she shops, she estimates the cost of the groceries so that she will have enough money when she goes to the cash register. She estimates that the groceries in her cart will cost about $32.

A. The actual cost of the groceries is $34.52. Is her estimate within 10% of the actual cost?

B. Is her estimate close enough? Explain.

168 SG • Grade 4 • Unit 6 • Lesson 5   Close Enough

Student Guide **- page 168** *(Answers on p. 90)*

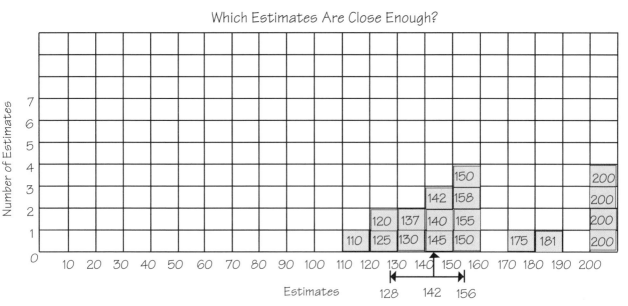

Figure 21: *All the estimates between 128 and 156 are within 10% of 142.*

At a Glance

Before the Activity

1. Students complete *Questions 8–10* of the Homework section of the previous lesson (Lesson 4 *News Number Line*). They make mystery jars by filling (or partly filling) jars with small objects and then bring the jars to class.
2. Fill a jar with 123 objects to use with discussion prompts as an example for finding 10%. (optional)
3. Fill a large and a small jar with objects to supplement the students' jars. (optional)

Part 1. Estimating the Number of Objects in Mystery Jars

1. Place your mystery jar and some of the students' mystery jars around the room with jars of a known number of objects to use as reference numbers.
2. Students estimate the number of objects in the jars and record their estimates in a table.
3. Use the discussion prompts to guide a discussion on what it means to have a close estimate.
4. Establish a general standard for closeness: An estimate is close if it is within 10% of the actual number.
5. Use the discussion prompts to describe how to find 10% of a number.
6. The class completes the *10% Chart* Activity Page in the *Discovery Assignment Book* to practice finding 10%. Students use the chart to look for patterns to help them find 10% easily.

Part 2. When Are Estimates Close Enough?

1. Students review and practice skills and concepts from Part 1 by discussing *Questions 1–7* on the *Close Enough* Activity Pages in the *Student Guide.*
2. Students repeat the estimation process using different mystery jars. (optional)
3. In *Question 8,* students estimate the height of a door and identify the estimates that are within 10% of the actual measurement.
4. In *Question 9,* students discuss a situation in which an error of 10% is not appropriate.

Homework

Assign the Homework section in the *Student Guide.*

Assessment

Use *Questions 1–2* in the Homework section as an assessment.

Extension

Make a bar graph like Figure 21 to help students identify estimates within 10%.

Connection

Practice estimation with books like those in the *Great Waldo Search* series.

Answer Key is on pages 88–90.

Notes:

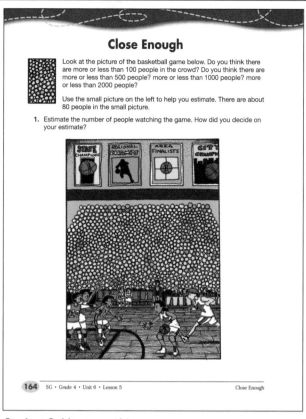

Student Guide - page 164

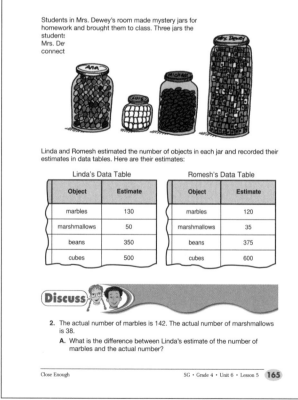

Student Guide - page 165

*Answers and/or discussion are included in the Lesson Guide.

Student Guide (p. 164)

Close Enough

1. Estimates will vary. The small picture fits into the larger picture about 11 times. $80 \times 11 = 880$ or about 900 people.

Student Guide (p. 165)

2. **A.** 12 marbles

Student Guide (p. 166)

B. 12 marshmallows

C. Yes. Linda's estimate is within 10% of the actual number of marbles, but it is not within 10% of the actual number of marshmallows.*

3. A. Linda's estimate*

B. Yes.

4.* A. Students' solution paths will vary. 10% of 38 is 3.8 or about 3 or 4.

B. Romesh's estimate.

B. What is the difference between Linda's estimate of the number of marshmallows and the actual number?

C. Is Linda's estimate for the number of marbles better than her estimate for the number of marshmallows? Why or why not?

 Mrs. Dewey said: "Let's say that an estimate is 'close enough' if it is within ten percent. Ten percent (10%) means 10 out of every 100. That's the same as 1 out of every 10 or $\frac{1}{10}$. So, to find out which numbers are within 10% of 142, we have to find $\frac{1}{10}$ of 142. How can we do that?"

Linda chose to find $\frac{1}{10}$ of 142 by dividing the marbles into 10 equal groups. When she finished, each group had 14 marbles, and two marbles were left over. She decided that $\frac{1}{10}$ of 142 is about 14.

 Romesh used a calculator to find $\frac{1}{10}$ of 142. He divided 142 by 10. Since the display read 14.2, he agreed with Linda: 10% of 142 is about 14.

Any prediction in the range between 128 and 156 is within 10% of 142, since:

$$142 - 14 = 128$$
and
$$142 + 14 = 156.$$

3. A. Look back at Linda's and Romesh's estimates listed in the data tables. Which of the estimates for the jar of marbles is within 10% of 142?

B. Do you agree that this estimate is close enough?

4. A. Find 10% of 38. Check your answer by finding 10% of 38 in a different way.

B. Look back at Linda's and Romesh's estimates listed in the data tables. Which of the estimates for the jar of marshmallows is within 10%?

166 SG • Grade 4 • Unit 6 • Lesson 5 Close Enough

Student Guide - page 166

Student Guide (p. 167)

5.

Object	N Actual Number	$N \div 10$	10% of the Number	Range
marbles	142	14.2	About 14	128–156
marshmallows	38	3.8	About 3 or 4	34–42
beans	351	35.1	About 35	316–386
cubes	526	52.6	About 52 or 53	473–579

6. A. Yes. Linda estimated 350 and the actual number of beans is 351.

B. Yes. The 10% range is from 316–386.

7. A. Yes. The 10% range is from 473–579.

B. No. Romesh's estimate is outside the 10% range.

8. A.–C. Answers will vary.

9. No. The door will not close or lock correctly if it is only within 10% of 75 cm. A door must be much closer to the actual measure of the opening.

---

5. Draw the following data table on your paper. Complete the table.

Object	N Actual Number	$N \div 10$	10% of the Number	Range
marbles	142	14.2	About 14	128–156
marshmallows	38			
beans	351			
cubes	526			

6. A. Is Linda's estimate for the number of beans within 10%? Why or why not?

B. Is the estimate Romesh made for the number of beans within 10%? Why or why not?

7. A. Is Linda's estimate for the number of cubes within 10%? Why or why not?

B. Is the estimate Romesh made for the number of cubes within 10%? Why or why not?

8. Estimate the height of the door to your classroom to the nearest cm.

A. Record your estimate and share it with your class.

B. Measure the height of the door to the nearest cm.

C. Which estimates are within 10% of the actual measurement?

9. A carpenter is making a door. The opening is 75 cm wide. If the carpenter measures the width of the door to within 10%, will the measurement be close enough? Why or why not?

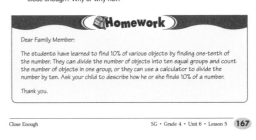

Homework

Dear Family Member:

The students have learned to find 10% of various objects by finding one-tenth of the number. They can divide the number of objects into ten equal groups and count the number of objects in one group, or they can use a calculator to divide the number by ten. Ask your child to describe how he or she finds 10% of a number.

Thank you.

Close Enough SG • Grade 4 • Unit 6 • Lesson 5 **167**

Student Guide - page 167

---

*Answers and/or discussion are included in the Lesson Guide.

1. Here is part of the *10% Chart* made by students in Mrs. Dewey's class. Complete the table.

Object	N Actual Number	N ÷ 10	10% of the Number	Range
blocks	51			
macaroni	632			
pennies	198			
Super Balls	15			

2. A. Is an estimate of 60 blocks within 10% of the actual number? Show how you know.

B. Is an estimate of 650 macaroni pieces within 10% of the actual number? Show how you know.

C. Is an estimate of 175 pennies within 10% of the actual number? Show how you know.

D. Is an estimate of 18 Super Balls within 10% of the actual number? Show how you know.

3. Tanya is working on the *Bouncing Ball* experiment. She predicts that the tennis ball will bounce to a height of 50 cm if it is dropped from a height of 100 cm. She checks her prediction, and the ball actually bounces to a height of 54 cm. Is her prediction of 50 cm within 10% of the actual bounce height of 54 cm? Why, or why not?

4. The average height of students in Room 204 is 55 inches. Nila is 48 inches tall. Is her height within 10% of the average height?

5. Keenya goes to the store with $32 for groceries. As she shops, she estimates the cost of the groceries so that she will have enough money when she goes to the cash register. She estimates that the groceries in her cart will cost about $32.

A. The actual cost of the groceries is $34.52. Is her estimate within 10% of the actual cost?

B. Is her estimate close enough? Explain.

Student Guide - page 168

Student Guide (p. 168)

Homework

1.

Object	N Actual Number	N ÷ 10	10% of the Number	Range
blocks	51	5.1	About 5	46–56
macaroni	632	63.2	About 63	569–695
pennies	198	19.8	About 20	178–218
Super balls	15	1.5	Between 1 and 2	13–17

2. A. No. Within 10% of 51 is the range 46–56.

B. Yes. The 10% range for 632 pieces of macaroni is 569–695.

C. No. The 10% range for 198 is 178–218.

D. No. The 10% range for 15 is 13–17.

3. Yes. The 10% range for 54 cm is 49–59 cm.

4. No. 10% of 55 is between 5 and 6 inches; 48 inches is 7 inches less than the average height.

5. A. Yes. 10% of $34.52 is between $3 and $4; $32 is only about $2 or $3 less than the actual price.

B. No. Keenya does not have enough money to buy the groceries.

Using Estimation

Lesson Overview

Estimated Class Sessions 2-3

Students use number lines to round numbers. They identify the different benchmarks to use when rounding numbers. Students recognize that the benchmarks they choose affect the accuracy and the ease of use of rounded numbers. They estimate sums and differences using rounded numbers and explore when it is appropriate to use an estimate. Students review the Student Rubric: *Knowing* as they write about estimation.

Key Content

- Using benchmarks to round numbers.
- Choosing appropriate convenient numbers.
- Estimating sums and differences of large numbers.

Key Vocabulary

- benchmark
- rounded number

Math Facts

DPP item M provides practice with math facts for the nines. Bit O is a short quiz on the multiplication facts for the nines.

Homework

1. Assign *Questions 1–4* in the Homework section after Part 1.
2. Assign *Questions 5–12* in the Homework section after Part 2.
3. Assign Parts 4 and 7 of the Home Practice.

Assessment

1. Students complete the skill assessment *Check-Up Time*.
2. Use DPP item O *Multiplication Quiz: 9s* as an assessment.
3. Use the Knowing dimension of the *TIMS Multidimensional Rubric* to assess students' abilities to use computational estimation.
4. Use the *Observational Assessment Record* to document students' abilities to represent larger numbers on number lines and estimate sums and differences.
5. Transfer appropriate documentation from the Unit 6 *Observational Assessment Record* to students' *Individual Assessment Record Sheets.*

Curriculum Sequence

Before This Unit

Estimation

In Grade 3 Unit 6, students used rounding to find convenient numbers. They then used convenient numbers to estimate answers in addition and subtraction problems. Students estimated sums and differences throughout the Daily Practice and Problems and Home Practice. See Grade 3.

Student Rubrics

Students used all the Student Rubrics (*Solving, Knowing,* and *Telling*) in third grade to help them describe their problem-solving strategies. The Student Rubric: *Knowing*, which is reviewed in this lesson, was introduced in Grade 3 Unit 2 and then used throughout the year.

The Student Rubric: *Solving* was reintroduced in Grade 4 Unit 5 and the Student Rubric: *Telling* was reintroduced in Grade 4 Unit 2.

After This Unit

Estimation

Students will continue to develop computational estimation skills in Unit 7.

Student Rubrics

Students will use the *Knowing* and *Solving* rubrics to help them solve a problem in Unit 7 Lesson 3. See the Lesson Guides for Unit 8 Lesson 5 and Unit 16 Lesson 4 for examples of students' work scored on a rubric.

Materials List

Supplies and Copies

Student	Teacher
Supplies for Each Student	**Supplies**
Copies • 1 copy of *Check-Up Time* per student (*Unit Resource Guide* Pages 102–103)	**Copies/Transparencies** • 1 copy of *TIMS Multidimensional Rubric* (*Teacher Implementation Guide,* Assessment section) • 1 transparency or poster of Student Rubric: *Knowing* (*Teacher Implementation Guide,* Assessment section) • 1 transparency of a blank number line, optional

All blackline masters including assessment, transparency, and DPP masters are also on the Teacher Resource CD.

Student Books
Using Estimation (*Student Guide* Pages 169–174)
Student Rubric: *Knowing* (*Student Guide* Appendix A and Inside Back Cover)

Daily Practice and Problems and Home Practice
DPP items M–P (*Unit Resource Guide* Pages 22–24)
Home Practice Parts 4 & 7 (*Discovery Assignment Book* Pages 68 & 70)

Note: Classrooms whose pacing differs significantly from the suggested pacing of the units should use the Math Facts Calendar in Section 4 of the *Facts Resource Guide* to ensure students receive the complete math facts program.

Assessment Tools
Observational Assessment Record (*Unit Resource Guide* Pages 11–12)
Individual Assessment Record Sheet (*Teacher Implementation Guide,* Assessment section)
TIMS Multidimensional Rubric (*Teacher Implementation Guide,* Assessment section)

Daily Practice and Problems

Suggestions for using the DPPs are on pages 98–99.

M. Bit: More Fine Nines (URG p. 22)

Do these problems in your head. Write the answers and then write the other number sentences in the same fact family.

A. $9 \times 3 =$ B. $9 \times 2 =$

C. $63 \div 9 =$ D. $8 \times 9 =$

E. $81 \div 9 =$ F. $9 \times 4 =$

G. $10 \times 9 =$ H. $54 \div 9 =$

I. $5 \times 9 =$

O. Bit: Multiplication Quiz: 9s (URG p. 24)

A. $3 \times 9 =$ B. $9 \times 7 =$

C. $10 \times 9 =$ D. $2 \times 9 =$

E. $5 \times 9 =$ F. $9 \times 8 =$

G. $6 \times 9 =$ H. $4 \times 9 =$

I. $9 \times 9 =$ J. $9 \times 1 =$

N. Challenge: Flying Rumors
(URG p. 23)

I.M. Polite told a rumor to two people on the first day of school. On the second day, the two people who heard the rumor each told the rumor to two more people. On the third day, the four people who heard the rumor on the second day each told it to two more people.

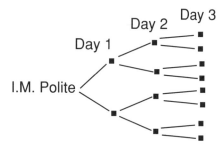

1. If this pattern is continued, how many new people will hear the rumor for the first time on the tenth day? How did you decide?

2. How many total people will know the rumor on the sixth day? How did you decide?

3. There are 500 people in the school. On what day will the whole school know the rumor? Show how you did this problem.

P. Task: Which Is Closest? (URG p. 24)

1. Which number is closest to 4056?
   450 4000 4100 5000

2. Which number is closest to 62,096?
   7000 60,000 65,000 70,000

3. Which is a reasonable estimate for the height of a 5-story apartment building?
   30 feet 50 feet 300 feet 500 feet

Make an overhead transparency of the Student
Rubric: *Knowing* or a poster of the rubric by enlarg-
ing the blackline master found in the Assessment
section of the *Teacher Implementation Guide.*
A transparency of a blank number line to use in
Part 1 of this lesson would also be helpful.

Teaching the Activity

Part 1 It's About . . .

Remove the newspaper clippings from the newswire
bulletin board. Divide students into small groups and
give each group a share of the news items. Ask each
group to sort the articles into two categories—those
that appear to be exact numbers and those that
appear to be rounded numbers. Remind students that
a **rounded number** is a number close to the exact
number, but is expressed to the nearest ten, hundred,
thousand, etc. After sorting is completed, talk about
what the students discovered from this activity.
Comments may include: The bigger numbers are not
usually exact numbers; smaller numbers are written
as exact numbers more often than larger numbers;
numbers greater than one million are often written in
text (such as 1.2 million).

Direct students to the *Using Estimation* Activity
Pages in the *Student Guide.* Read the short vignette,
It's About. . . . Invite students to share strategies for
estimating the sum of the numbers. Introduce the use
of a number line to find rounded numbers. Work
through *Questions 1–6* together. Use the transparency
of a number line as you answer these questions.

In *Question 1,* students find a rounded number for
407,997 that is expressed to the nearest hundred thousand. Students are asked to identify **benchmarks** that
they use as they round 407,997. *Question 2* asks students to find a rounded number for 458,156 expressed
to the nearest hundred thousand. They will once again
identify benchmarks. Note that the benchmarks for
rounding 458,156 to the nearest 100,000 are the same
as those used to round 407,997 to the nearest 100,000.

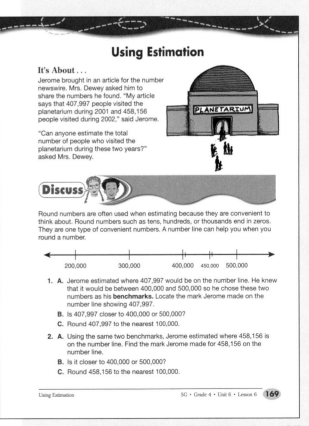

Using Estimation

It's About . . .
Jerome brought in an article for the number
newswire. Mrs. Dewey asked him to
share the numbers he found. "My article
says that 407,997 people visited the
planetarium during 2001 and 458,156
people visited during 2002," said Jerome.

"Can anyone estimate the total
number of people who visited the
planetarium during these two years?"
asked Mrs. Dewey.

Discuss

Round numbers are often used when estimating because they are convenient to
think about. Round numbers such as tens, hundreds, or thousands end in zeros.
They are one type of convenient numbers. A number line can help you when you
round a number.

1. **A.** Jerome estimated where 407,997 would be on the number line. He knew
    that it would be between 400,000 and 500,000 so he chose these two
    numbers as his **benchmarks.** Locate the mark Jerome made on the
    number line showing 407,997.
   B. Is 407,997 closer to 400,000 or 500,000?
   C. Round 407,997 to the nearest 100,000.

2. **A.** Using the same two benchmarks, Jerome estimated where 458,156 is
    on the number line. Find the mark Jerome made for 458,156 on the
    number line.
   B. Is it closer to 400,000 or 500,000?
   C. Round 458,156 to the nearest 100,000.

Using Estimation   SG • Grade 4 • Unit 6 • Lesson 6 **169**

Student Guide - page 169 *(Answers on p. 104)*

3. Ana did not round 458,156 to the nearest hundred thousand. She rounded 458,156 in two other ways. She used these two number lines.

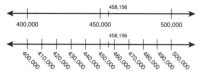

Using these two number lines, give two ways to round 458,156.

4. A. Ana used the second number line in Question 3 to round 407,997 to the nearest 10,000. What is her estimate?

B. What benchmarks did she use?

5. Jerome estimated the total number of people who visited the planetarium over the last two years as 900,000. Ana's estimate was 870,000 people.

A. Write a number sentence to show how Jerome found his estimate.

B. Write a number sentence to show how Ana found her estimate.

C. Which student is correct?

6. The museum estimated how much the attendance grew from 2001 to 2002. Use rounded numbers to estimate the increase in attendance.

Practice rounding the numbers in each problem below.

7. A. Use this number line to round 8207 to the nearest thousand.

B. What two benchmarks did you use?

8. A. Round 8207 to the nearest hundred using this number line.

Student Guide - page 170 *(Answers on p. 104)*

B. What two benchmarks did you use?

C. Compare this rounded number with the rounded number you found in Question 7. Which one is closer to the exact number?

D. Last year, 8207 people attended a high school play. The school play committee is expecting about the same number to attend this year's show. If the committee members are trying to plan refreshments for this year's show, which rounded number would be best to use?

9. A. Use this number line to round 36,736 to the nearest thousand.

B. What two benchmarks did you use?

C. Round 36,736 to the nearest 10,000. Draw a number line showing the benchmarks you would use.

D. Last year 36,736 tickets were sold at a fun fair during a summer festival. The planning committee is getting ready to order tickets for this summer's fun fair. Tickets are sold in rolls of 1000. If the planning committee expects about the same number of tickets to be sold, which rounded number should they use when ordering the tickets?

Estimating Sums and Differences

Ming and Keenya were researching the national parks in the United States. They found that Yellowstone National Park, established in 1872, was the world's first national park. Since then, more than 50 national parks have been set aside by the American government.

Student Guide - page 171 *(Answers on p. 105)*

In **Question 3,** 458,156 is rounded first to the nearest 50,000 (450,000) and then to the nearest 10,000 (460,000). Both estimates are acceptable. Discuss which estimate is more accurate.

Question 5 returns to the original question posed in the vignette: Estimate the number of people who visited the planetarium over the two years. In this question, Jerome and Ana both give an estimate based on the convenient numbers they chose. While Ana's estimate (410,000 + 460,000 = 870,000) is more accurate, the numbers that Jerome used (400,000 + 500,000 = 900,000) are somewhat easier to add using mental math. However, both students' answers are acceptable. Allow time to discuss when accuracy is desirable and when it is okay to choose numbers that are easier to use. **Question 6** provides an opportunity to round numbers to estimate the answer to a subtraction problem.

Content Note

Round Numbers. Traditionally, students were taught to round numbers in a very procedural way, i.e., there is one set of rules for rounding. The emphasis of this lesson is to help students choose convenient numbers that will help them make logical estimates. Usually there will be several different choices of convenient numbers that make sense.

Questions 7–9 provide additional practice rounding numbers. Have students work with a partner. This will allow them to compare answers and receive immediate feedback on their work. **Questions 8D and 9D** ask students to determine how accurate one needs to be in two different situations. The context of a problem often dictates the decisions that must be made when estimating. In these cases, it is probably better to overestimate the amount of food and tickets to order—having too few tickets or not enough food would cause problems. Ordering too much, however, would be a wasted expense. Discuss these issues as you decide what appropriate estimates would be.

Assign homework **Questions 1–4.** These questions provide independent practice rounding large numbers.

Part 2 Estimating Sums and Differences

One reason we use rounded numbers is to estimate approximate answers when we add, subtract, multiply, or divide. The Estimating Sums and Differences section of the *Using Estimation* Activity Pages in the *Student Guide* provides students with a context for using rounded numbers to add and subtract. Read the short vignette about Ming and Keenya. Look at the information contained in the National Parks table.

In **Question 10,** Ming has estimated that there are about 1,300,000 acres of land set aside in Arizona as national park land. Ming has written a number sentence showing the rounded numbers that he chose. Students are asked to tell how Ming arrived at his estimate. Students should see that he rounded the acreages of the two Arizona national parks in the chart to the nearest hundred thousand. He then added these together. In **Question 10B,** students are asked to suggest a different estimate for this question. If students round 1,217,403 to the nearest hundred thousand and 93,533 to the nearest ten thousand they may suggest that there are about 1,290,000 acres of land set aside in Arizona. Students might also round both numbers to the nearest ten thousand, suggesting that there are about 1,310,000 acres of land set aside in Arizona. Each of these estimates is acceptable.

Questions 11–13 provide additional practice with estimating sums and differences. Students are to write a number sentence showing how they found each estimate. All reasonable estimates should be accepted.

Assign homework **Questions 5–12** after completing this section. **Questions 5–10** give independent practice using a paper-and-pencil method for adding and subtracting. This reviews previously learned material. Students are asked to estimate to see if their answers are reasonable. Ask students to write the number sentence they used to estimate each answer. **Question 11** asks students to use figures in the length of the coastlines of the United States.

Part 3 Making Money

Use **Question 14** in the *Student Guide* to review the Student Rubric: *Knowing* with students. Begin by reading the short vignette that gives the context for this problem. Read the problem together and discuss what is being asked. Help students plan their paragraphs using the Student Rubric: *Knowing.* Use the following prompts as you discuss the rubric and the assignment:

* *How can you show that you understand what this problem is asking?*

* *What are some different ways you can show the mathematical ideas you used to solve this problem?*

* *What tools can you use to solve this problem? How can you show that you know how to use these tools?*

* *How can you show the facts and procedures that you used to solve this problem?*

After students complete their work, use the student rubric to help them assess it. Provide feedback that will help them revise their work.

Ming used a table to organize some of the national park information they found.

National Parks

National Park	State	Established	Area
Acadia	Maine	1929	46,051 acres
Badlands	South Dakota	1978	242,756 acres
Carlsbad Caverns	New Mexico	1930	46,776 acres
Denali	Alaska	1980	4,740,911 acres
Everglades	Florida	1934	1,398,902 acres
Grand Canyon	Arizona	1919	1,217,403 acres
Mammoth Cave	Kentucky	1941	52,830 acres
Mesa Verde	Colorado	1906	52,122 acres
Petrified Forest	Arizona	1962	93,533 acres
Rocky Mountains	Colorado	1915	265,769 acres
Wind Cave	South Dakota	1903	28,295 acres

10. **A.** Ming estimated that about 1,300,000 acres of land have been set aside in Arizona as national park land. Ming wrote this number sentence showing the convenient numbers he chose:

   1,200,000 + 100,000 = 1,300,000 acres of land set aside

   Explain how Ming arrived at his estimate.

   B. Find another estimate for the amount of land set aside in Arizona as national park land. Explain your thinking.

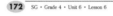

Use Ming and Keenya's table to answer Questions 11–13. Write a number sentence showing the convenient numbers you chose to use.

11. Estimate the amount of land set aside in Colorado as national park land.

12. Which state, Arizona or Colorado, has more national park land? Estimate the difference.

13. Mammoth Cave is the longest known cave network in the world. Estimate the difference in size between Mammoth Cave National Park and Wind Cave National Park.

Student Guide - page 172 *(Answers on p. 105)*

Making Money

The Parent-Teacher Committee at Bessie Coleman School wants to purchase computer hardware for the school computer lab over a two-year period. The committee's goal is to purchase hardware for 25 computer lab stations. Committee members made a table to show what they wanted to buy:

Quantity	Item	Total Cost ($)
25	14-inch color monitor	7469.00
25	extended keyboards	3127.00
25	personal computers	30,716.00
25	color printers	14,054.00

14. Use estimation to set a goal for the amount of money the Parent-Teacher Committee needs to earn. Write a paragraph explaining how you arrived at your goal. Use the Student Rubric: *Knowing* to help you write your paragraph.

1. Find at least two ways to round each of these numbers.
   • Draw a number line for each rounded number.
   • Label your line with the benchmarks you chose.
   • Estimate the location of the actual number on the number line.

   A. 5599   B. 24,681   C. 18,260

   D. 764,296   E. 206,492   F. 6,847,000

Use this number line to answer Questions 2–4.

```
◄──┼──────┼──────┼──────┼──────┼──►
1,500,000  1,600,000  1,700,000  1,800,000  1,900,000
```

2. According to an article Linda hung on the newswire, 1,858,766 people visited the aquarium last year. Use the number line to round 1,858,766 to the nearest hundred thousand.

Student Guide - page 173 *(Answers on p. 106)*

Think about using numbers. Describe at least two occasions when it is important to use exact numbers and two occasions when it is okay to use rounded numbers.

Look for the following as you help students revise their work:

- *Did students show understanding of the problem by using estimation to set their goal instead of exact computation?*

- *Did students explain their answers in more than one way? For example, did they represent the convenient numbers they chose in number sentences as well as in tables? Or did students draw number lines to show how they chose convenient numbers?*

- *Did students choose to use a calculator and if so was it used correctly?*

- *Did convenient numbers lead to a reasonable goal? Is the addition correct?*

Once students revise their work, have them share their solutions with other students. Hearing how others solve a problem will often help students refine their own thinking.

Math Facts

DPP Bit M provides practice for the math facts for the nines.

Homework and Practice

- Students can complete **Questions 1–4** in the Homework section on the *Using Estimation* Activity Pages in the *Student Guide* after completing Part 1 of the lesson.
- Homework **Questions 5–12** can be assigned after completing Part 2.
- DPP Task P provides practice with estimation and rounding skills developed in this unit.
- Parts 4 and 7 of the Home Practice ask students to estimate and round with large numbers.

Answers for Parts 4 and 7 of the Home Practice are in the Answer Key at the end of this lesson and at the end of this unit.

Assessment

- A four-item quiz, *Check-Up Time,* has been included in the *Unit Resource Guide* as a skill assessment.
- Use DPP Bit O to assess students' fluency with the multiplication facts for the nines.

---

3. In one year, 1,510,063 people visited the Sears Tower Skydeck. Use the number line to round 1,510,063 to the nearest hundred thousand.

4. During one season, a total of 1,697,398 people attended home games for the Chicago White Sox. Use the number line to round 1,697,398 to the nearest hundred thousand.

Addition and Subtraction Practice with Paper and Pencil

Solve the following problems using paper and pencil. Find exact answers. Show all your work. Use estimation to look back and see if your answers are reasonable.

5. 9436
   + 4831

6. 4302
   + 3005

7. 7407
   − 3822

Estimate the answers to the following problems. Show the round numbers you used.

8. 23,065
   − 9,638

9. 94,378
   − 76,893

10. 80,025
    − 9,559

11. The United States has 12,383 miles of coastline along four different oceans. The Atlantic coast is 2069 miles long, the Arctic coast is 1060 miles long, and the coast of the Gulf of Mexico is 1631 miles long. About how long is the Pacific coast of the United States?

12. The United States has a total area of 3,787,319 square miles. Water covers 251,041 square miles. About how much of the United States area is land?

Student Guide - page 174 (Answers on p. 107)

Use **Question 14** in the Making Money section of the *Using Estimation* Activity Pages to assess your students' facility with computational estimation. Students must write a paragraph explaining their estimation strategies. Review the Student Rubric: *Knowing* so students can use it to guide their work on the problem. Use the Knowing dimension of the *TIMS Multidimensional Rubric* to score students' work.

- Use the *Observational Assessment Record* to document students' abilities to represent large numbers on number lines and estimate sums and differences using large numbers.

- Transfer appropriate documentation from the Unit 6 *Observational Assessment Record* to students' *Individual Assessment Record Sheets*.

Extension

DPP item N is a challenging problem that uses the same concepts and skills as the problem in Lesson 2 *Doubles*.

Literature Connection

- McKissack, Patricia. *A Million Fish . . . More or Less.* Alfred A. Knopf, New York, 1996.

  In this story, a young boy first catches three small fish and then a million more. As he tries to bring the fish home, he loses them to the gators, the raccoons, and a hungry cat. When he arrives home, he has just enough fish for supper and a whopping "fish story" to share with his family. This story would be appropriate to read aloud during Part 2 of this lesson.

- Schwartz, David. *How Much Is a Million?* William Morrow and Company, New York, 1993.

Social Sciences Connection

You can link the information about our national parks in this lesson and in Lesson 1 with studies of United States geography. You may want to show students a map of the United States before assigning the homework. **Question 11** involves the length of the coastlines.

Name _____ Date _____

PART 3 Addition and Subtraction Practice
Use paper and pencil to solve the following problems. Use estimation to decide if your answers make sense. Explain your estimation strategy for F.

A.	4506 + 8753	B.	5388 + 9078	C.	9054 − 2408

D.	7617 − 4543	E.	3940 + 6963	F.	10,415 − 7593

PART 4 Using Estimation
The following table lists the number of people who immigrated to the United States from various countries in 2000. Use the information in the table to estimate the answers to the questions below. Use a separate sheet of paper to show what convenient numbers you chose to work with.

Country	Number of Immigrants	Country	Number of Immigrants
Canada	21,475	Mexico	171,748
China	41,861	Philippines	40,587
Dominican Republic	17,441	Romania	6,521
El Salvador	22,332	United Kingdom	14,532
India	39,072	Vietnam	25,340

1. Most immigrants came from which five countries listed in the table? List the countries and their number of immigrants. List the number of immigrants in order from largest to smallest.

2. About how many more people immigrated from Mexico than from China?

3. About how many people immigrated from Canada and Mexico combined?

4. The number of immigrants from El Salvador is about the same as the number from which other country?

5. About how many more people came from India than Romania?

6. In 2000, the number of immigrants from all countries totaled about 850,000 people. About how many immigrants are reported in the table above? (*Hint:* Use a calculator to help you with your estimation.)

Discovery Assignment Book - page 68 (Answers on p. 107)

Name _____ Date _____

PART 6 Subtraction Count Backs
Do these problems in your head. Write only the answers. Work across the rows.

A. $11 - 2 =$ _____   B. $31 - 2 =$ _____
C. $110 - 20 =$ _____   D. $310 - 20 =$ _____
E. $27 - 3 =$ _____   F. $7 - 3 =$ _____
G. $2700 - 300 =$ _____   H. $70 - 30 =$ _____
I. $12 - 3 =$ _____   J. $52 - 3 =$ _____
K. $120 - 30 =$ _____   L. $5200 - 300 =$ _____

Describe any patterns you see.

PART 7 Convenient Numbers
Estimate where each of the numbers (A–D) is located on the following number line. Make a mark on the number line to show each number. Label each mark with the correct letter A, B, C, or D. Then use the number line to round each number to the nearest ten thousand and nearest hundred thousand.

500,000   600,000   700,000   800,000   900,000

Nearest ten thousand   Nearest hundred thousand

A. 650,780 _____   _____
B. 870,002 _____   _____
C. 720,000 _____   _____
D. 509,237 _____   _____

Discovery Assignment Book - page 70 (Answers on p. 108)

At a Glance

Math Facts and Daily Practice and Problems
DPP item M provides practice with math facts for the nines. Item N is a challenging problem. Bit O is a short quiz on the multiplication facts for the nines. Task P develops number sense for large numbers.

Part 1. It's About . . .
1. Divide the class into small groups. Take numbers from the newswire. Give a selection of articles to each group.
2. Review the definition of round numbers.
3. Sort the numbers from the newswire and articles from Lesson 1 into two groups, those that appear to be exact and those that appear to be rounded.
4. Discuss student observations about the numbers they sorted.
5. Read the It's About . . . vignette on the *Using Estimation* Activity Pages in the *Student Guide.*
6. Work with the large group to answer *Questions 1–6* in the *Student Guide.* Make sure students understand that a number can be rounded in more than one way.
7. Students complete *Questions 7–9* in pairs. Allow time for students to discuss their solutions and their strategies.

Part 2. Estimating Sums and Differences
1. Use the Estimating Sums and Differences vignette in the *Student Guide* to provide a context for adding and subtracting convenient numbers.
2. Discuss *Question 10.* Provide an opportunity for students to share strategies.
3. Have students use the data chart of national park information to complete *Questions 11–13.*

Part 3. Making Money
1. After reading the short vignette, students review the Student Rubric: *Knowing.*
2. Students answer *Question 14,* which involves computational estimation and writing an explanation.
3. Students use the rubric to assess their own work.
4. Students revise their work based on their self-assessment and teacher feedback.

Homework
1. Assign *Questions 1–4* in the Homework section after Part 1.
2. Assign *Questions 5–12* in the Homework section after Part 2.
3. Assign Parts 4 and 7 of the Home Practice.

Assessment
1. Students complete the skill assessment *Check-Up Time.*
2. Use DPP item O *Multiplication Quiz: 9s* as an assessment.
3. Use the Knowing dimension of the *TIMS Multidimensional Rubric* to assess students' abilities to use computational estimation.
4. Use the *Observational Assessment Record* to document students' abilities to represent larger numbers on number lines and estimate sums and differences.
5. Transfer appropriate documentation from the Unit 6 *Observational Assessment Record* to students' *Individual Assessment Record Sheets.*

At a Glance

Extension

Use DPP item N to challenge students with the concepts and skills used in Lesson 2.

Connection

1. Share *A Million Fish . . . More or Less* or *How Much Is a Million?* with students.
2. Connect this lesson with social studies through discussion of national parks data and geography.

Answer Key is on pages 104–109.

Notes:

Check-Up Time

Use the skills and strategies you learned in this unit to help you answer these questions.

1. The number of papers sold on Sunday for five local newspapers is listed in the chart.

Sunday Newspaper Circulation

Newspaper	Number of Papers Sold on Sunday
Daily Herald	122,441
Munster Times	78,491
Daily Southtown	65,203
Post-Tribune	80,974
Northwest Herald	32,214

A. Put the numbers in order from smallest to largest.

B. Which number is closest to 100,000?

C. Estimate the combined number of Sunday papers sold by the Northwest Herald and the Daily Herald. Explain the strategies you used to find your estimate. Include a number sentence.

D. About how many more Sunday papers were sold by the Munster Times than the Northwest Herald?

2. Use patterns to complete the chart below.

1	1	1	one
10	10^1	10×1	
100			
1,000		$10 \times 10 \times 10$	
10,000	10^4		ten thousand
100,000			
1,000,000			

3. Write the following number using words: 348,603.

4. A state park reported that 1,688,489 people visited in 2000. In 2001, the park reported that 1,719,107 people visited. Estimate the total number of people who visited during these two years. Explain the strategy you used to make your estimate. Include a number sentence.

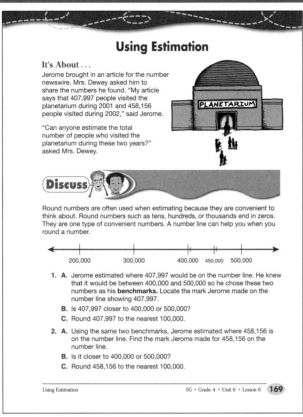

Student Guide - page 169

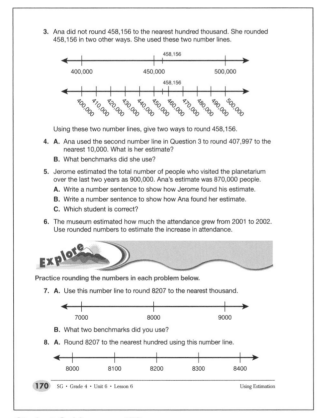

Student Guide - page 170

*Answers and/or discussion are included in the Lesson Guide.

Student Guide (p. 169)

Using Estimation

1. **A.**

   B. 400,000

   C. 400,000

2. **A.**

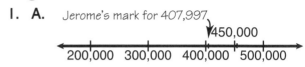

   B. 500,000

   C. 500,000

Student Guide (p. 170)

3. 450,000 or 460,000*

4. **A.** 410,000

   B. 400,000 and 410,000

5.* **A.** 400,000 + 500,000 = 900,000

   B. 410,000 + 460,000 = 870,000

   C. Both students are correct. Jerome's estimate is easier to compute. Ana's is more exact.

6. Estimates will vary. If rounding to ten thousands, then the attendance grew about 50,000.

7. **A.** 8000

   B. 8000 and 9000

8. **A.** 8200

Student Guide (p. 171)

B. 8200 and 8300

C. 8200 is closer.

D. 8200*

9. **A.** 37,000

B. 36,000 and 37,000

C. 40,000

37,736

30,000   40,000

D. 37,000*

B. What two benchmarks did you use?

C. Compare this rounded number with the rounded number you found in Question 7. Which one is closer to the exact number?

D. Last year, 8207 people attended a high school play. The school play committee is expecting about the same number to attend this year's show. If the committee members are trying to plan refreshments for this year's show, which rounded number would be best to use?

9. **A.** Use this number line to round 36,736 to the nearest thousand.

33,000   34,000   35,000   36,000   37,000   38,000

B. What two benchmarks did you use?

C. Round 36,736 to the nearest 10,000. Draw a number line showing the benchmarks you would use.

D. Last year 36,736 tickets were sold at a fun fair during a summer festival. The planning committee is getting ready to order tickets for this summer's fun fair. Tickets are sold in rolls of 1000. If the planning committee expects about the same number of tickets to be sold, which rounded number should they use when ordering the tickets?

Estimating Sums and Differences

Discuss

Ming and Keenya were researching the national parks in the United States. They found that Yellowstone National Park, established in 1872, was the world's first national park. Since then, more than 50 national parks have been set aside by the American government.

Using Estimation   SG • Grade 4 • Unit 6 • Lesson 6   **171**

Student Guide - page 171

Student Guide (p. 172)

10.* **A.** Explanations will vary. Ming rounded to the nearest hundred thousand.

B. Estimates will vary. One possible solution is to round to the nearest 10,000; 1,220,000 + 90,000 = 1,310,000 acres.

11. Estimates will vary. One possible solution is to round to the nearest 10,000; 50,000 + 270,000 = 320,000 acres.

12. Arizona. One possible solution is to round to the nearest 10,000; 1,310,000 − 320,000 is about 990,000 or about 1,000,000 acres.

13. Answers will vary. One possible solution is to round to the nearest 10,000; 50,000 − 30,000 = 20,000 acres.

Ming used a table to organize some of the national park information they found.

National Parks

National Park	State	Established	Area
Acadia	Maine	1929	46,051 acres
Badlands	South Dakota	1978	242,756 acres
Carlsbad Caverns	New Mexico	1930	46,776 acres
Denali	Alaska	1980	4,740,911 acres
Everglades	Florida	1934	1,398,902 acres
Grand Canyon	Arizona	1919	1,217,403 acres
Mammoth Cave	Kentucky	1941	52,830 acres
Mesa Verde	Colorado	1906	52,122 acres
Petrified Forest	Arizona	1962	93,533 acres
Rocky Mountains	Colorado	1915	265,769 acres
Wind Cave	South Dakota	1903	28,295 acres

10. **A.** Ming estimated that about 1,300,000 acres of land have been set aside in Arizona as national park land. Ming wrote this number sentence showing the convenient numbers he chose:

1,200,000 + 100,000 = 1,300,000 acres of land set aside

Explain how Ming arrived at his estimate.

B. Find another estimate for the amount of land set aside in Arizona as national park land. Explain your thinking.

Explore

Use Ming and Keenya's table to answer Questions 11–13. Write a number sentence showing the convenient numbers you chose to use.

11. Estimate the amount of land set aside in Colorado as national park land.

12. Which state, Arizona or Colorado, has more national park land? Estimate the difference.

13. Mammoth Cave is the longest known cave network in the world. Estimate the difference in size between Mammoth Cave National Park and Wind Cave National Park.

172   SG • Grade 4 • Unit 6 • Lesson 6   Using Estimation

Student Guide - page 172

*Answers and/or discussion are included in the Lesson Guide.

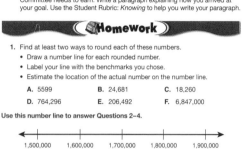

Student Guide - page 173

Student Guide (p. 173)

14. Estimates will vary. Rounding to the nearest thousand will yield: $55,000 ($7000 + $3000 + $31,000 + $14,000 = $55,000). However, since this is a cost estimate, it may be necessary to overestimate. A choice which is easy to compute: $8000 + $3000 + $30,000 + $15,000 = $56,000. Students should justify their choices.*

Homework

Answers will vary for *Question 1.* Two possible solutions are shown for each.

1. A. 6000

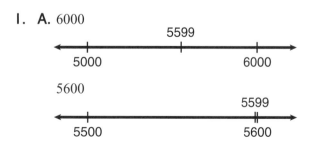

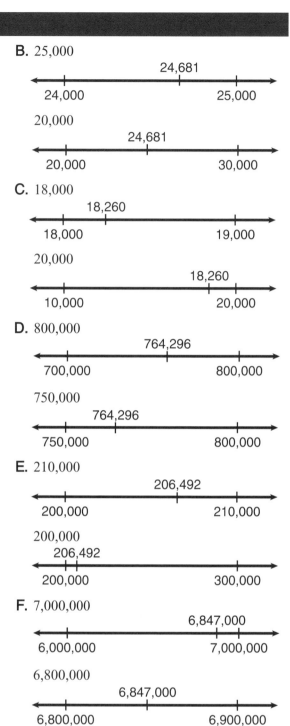

2. 1,900,000

*Answers and/or discussion are included in the Lesson Guide.

Student Guide (p. 174)

3. 1,500,000

4. 1,700,000

5. 14,267

6. 7307

7. 3585

8. Answers will vary. One possible solution is: 20,000 − 10,000 = 10,000.

9. Answers will vary. One possible solution is: 95,000 − 75,000 = 20,000.

10. Answers will vary. One possible solution is: 80,000 − 10,000 = 70,000.

11. Answers will vary. About 7000 miles.

12. Answers will vary. About 3,500,000 square miles.

3. In one year, 1,510,063 people visited the Sears Tower Skydeck. Use the number line to round 1,510,063 to the nearest hundred thousand.

4. During one season, a total of 1,697,398 people attended home games for the Chicago White Sox. Use the number line to round 1,697,398 to the nearest hundred thousand.

Addition and Subtraction Practice with Paper and Pencil

Solve the following problems using paper and pencil. Find exact answers. Show all your work. Use estimation to look back and see if your answers are reasonable.

| 5. 9436 + 4831 | 6. 4302 + 3005 | 7. 7407 − 3822 |

Estimate the answers to the following problems. Show the round numbers you used.

| 8. 23,065 − 9,638 | 9. 94,378 − 76,893 | 10. 80,025 − 9,559 |

11. The United States has 12,383 miles of coastline along four different oceans. The Atlantic coast is 2069 miles long, the Arctic coast is 1060 miles long, and the Gulf of Mexico is 1631 miles long. About how long is the Pacific coast of the United States?

12. The United States has a total area of 3,787,319 square miles. Water covers 251,041 square miles. About how much of the United States area is land?

174 SG • Grade 4 • Unit 6 • Lesson 6   Using Estimation

Student Guide - page 174

Discovery Assignment Book (p. 68)

Home Practice*

Part 4. Using Estimation

1. Mexico: 171,748; China: 41,861; Philippines: 40,587; India 39,072; Vietnam: 25,340

2. Answers will vary. One possible solution is: 130,000; 170,000 − 40,000 = 130,000 people.

3. Answers will vary. One possible solution is: 190,000; 20,000 + 170,000 = 190,000 people.

4. Canada

5. Answers will vary. One possible solution is: 30,000. 40,000 − 10,000 = 30,000 people.

6. Answers will vary based on estimates. One possible solution is 20,000 + 40,000 + 20,000 + 20,000 + 40,000 + 170,000 + 40,000 + 10,000 + 10,000 + 30,000 = 400,000 immigrants.

Name _____ Date _____

PART 3 **Addition and Subtraction Practice**
Use paper and pencil to solve the following problems. Use estimation to decide if your answers make sense. Explain your estimation strategy for F.

| A. 4506 + 8753 | B. 5388 + 9078 | C. 9054 − 2408 |
| D. 7617 − 4543 | E. 3940 + 6963 | F. 10,415 − 7593 |

PART 4 **Using Estimation**
The following table lists the number of people who immigrated to the United States from various countries in 2000. Use the information in the table to estimate the answers to the questions below. Use a separate sheet of paper to show what convenient numbers you chose to work with.

Country	Number of Immigrants	Country	Number of Immigrants
Canada	21,475	Mexico	171,748
China	41,861	Philippines	40,587
Dominican Republic	17,441	Romania	6,521
El Salvador	22,332	United Kingdom	14,532
India	39,072	Vietnam	25,340

1. Most immigrants came from which five countries listed in the table? List the countries and their number of immigrants. List the number of immigrants in order from largest to smallest.

2. About how many more people immigrated from Mexico than from China?

3. About how many people immigrated from Canada and Mexico combined?

4. The number of immigrants from El Salvador is about the same as the number from which other country?

5. About how many more people came from India than from Romania?

6. In 2000, the number of immigrants from all countries totaled about 850,000 people. About how many immigrants are reported in the table above? (*Hint:* Use a calculator to help you with your estimation.)

68 DAB • Grade 4 • Unit 6   PLACE VALUE PATTERNS

Discovery Assignment Book - page 68

*Answers for all the Home Practice in the *Discovery Assignment Book* are at the end of the unit.

Name _____ Date _____

PART 6 **Subtraction Count Backs**

Do these problems in your head. Write only the answers. Work across the rows.

A. 11 – 2 = _____   B. 31 – 2 = _____

C. 110 – 20 = _____   D. 310 – 20 = _____

E. 27 – 3 = _____   F. 7 – 3 = _____

G. 2700 – 300 = _____ H. 70 – 30 = _____

I. 12 – 3 = _____   J. 52 – 3 = _____

K. 120 – 30 = _____   L. 5200 – 300 = _____

Describe any patterns you see.

PART 7 **Convenient Numbers**

Estimate where each of the numbers (A–D) is located on the following number line. Make a mark on the number line to show each number. Label each mark with the correct letter A, B, C, or D. Then use the number line to round each number to the nearest ten thousand and nearest hundred thousand.

```
    500,000   600,000   700,000   800,000   900,000
```

	Nearest ten thousand	Nearest hundred thousand
A. 650,780	_____	_____
B. 870,002	_____	_____
C. 720,000	_____	_____
D. 509,237	_____	_____

Discovery Assignment Book - page 70

Discovery Assignment Book (p. 70)

Home Practice*

Part 7. Convenient Numbers

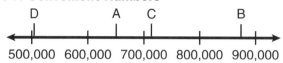

```
       D           A    C              B
  ←————|————|————|————|————|————|————|————→
     500,000 600,000 700,000 800,000 900,000
```

A. 650,000; 700,000

B. 870,000; 900,000

C. 720,000; 700,000

D. 510,000; 500,000

Name _____ Date _____

Check-Up Time

Use the skills and strategies you learned in this unit to help you answer these questions.

1. The number of papers sold on Sunday for five local newspapers is listed in the chart.

Sunday Newspaper Circulation

Newspaper	Number of Papers Sold on Sunday
Daily Herald	122,441
Munster Times	78,491
Daily Southtown	65,203
Post-Tribune	80,974
Northwest Herald	32,214

A. Put the numbers in order from smallest to largest.

B. Which number is closest to 100,000?

C. Estimate the combined number of Sunday papers sold by the Northwest Herald and the Daily Herald. Explain the strategies you used to find your estimate. Include a number sentence.

D. About how many more Sunday papers were sold by the Munster Times than the Northwest Herald?

Unit Resource Guide - page 102

Unit Resource Guide (p. 102)

Check-Up Time

I. **A.** 32,214; 65,203; 78,491; 80,974; 122,441

B. Post Tribune: 80,974

C. Answers will vary. One possible solution is to round to the nearest ten thousand: 30,000 + 120,000 = 150,000 newspapers.

D. Answers will vary. One possible solution is to round to the nearest 10,000: 80,000 − 30,000 = 50,000 newspapers.

---

*Answers for all the Home Practice in the *Discovery Assignment Book* are at the end of the unit.

Unit Resource Guide (p. 103)

2.

1	1	1	one
10	10^1	10×1	ten
100	10^2	10×10	one hundred
1,000	10^3	$10 \times 10 \times 10$	one thousand
10,000	10^4	$10 \times 10 \times 10 \times 10$	ten thousand
100,000	10^5	$10 \times 10 \times 10 \times 10 \times 10$	one hundred thousand
1,000,000	10^6	$10 \times 10 \times 10 \times 10 \times 10 \times 10$	one million

3. three hundred forty-eight thousand, six hundred three

4. Answers will vary. One possible solution is to round to the nearest hundred thousand: $1,700,000 + 1,700,000 = 3,400,000,$

Name _____ Date _____

2. Use patterns to complete the chart below.

1	1	1	one
10	10^1	10×1	
100			
1,000		$10 \times 10 \times 10$	
10,000	10^4		ten thousand
100,000			
1,000,000			

3. Write the following number using words: 348,603.

4. A state park reported that 1,688,489 people visited in 2000. In 2001, the park reported that 1,719,107 people visited. Estimate the total number of people who visited during these two years. Explain the strategy you used to make your estimate. Include a number sentence.

STATE PARK
Please Do Not Feed Wildlife

Copyright © Kendall/Hunt Publishing Company

Assessment Blackline Master   URG • Grade 4 • Unit 6 • Lesson 6   103

Unit Resource Guide - page 103

9 to 5 War

Estimated Class Sessions

1

Lesson Overview

Students play a card game that concentrates on the multiplication facts for the fives and nines.

Key Content

• Maintaining fluency with the multiplication facts for the 5s and 9s.

Key Vocabulary

• product

Math Facts

The *9 to 5 War* Game provides practice with multiplication facts for the fives and nines.

Homework

Ask students to play the game at home.

Materials List

Supplies and Copies

Student	Teacher
Supplies for Each Student Pair • scissors • calculator • deck of playing cards with face cards removed, optional	**Supplies**
Copies • 2 copies of *Digit Cards 0–9* per student copied back to back (*Unit Resource Guide* Pages 61–2) • 1 table from *Small Multiplication Tables* per student (*Unit Resource Guide* Page 115)	**Copies/Transparencies**

All blackline masters including assessment, transparency, and DPP masters are also on the Teacher Resource CD.

Student Books

9 to 5 War (*Student Guide* Pages 175–177)
9 to 5 War Cards (*Discovery Assignment Book* Pages 79–82)

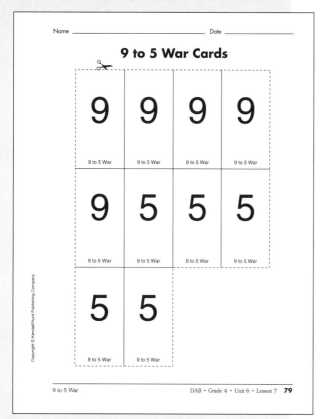

Discovery Assignment Book - page 79

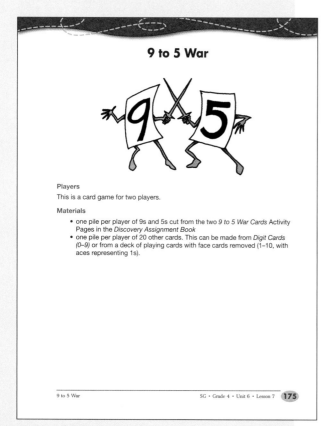

Student Guide - page 175

Before the Activity

Each student needs two stacks of cards: one stack of 9s and 5s and another stack of cards with other digits. Students cut out the two pages of *9 to 5 War Cards* provided in the *Discovery Assignment Book*. Each student will have 20 cards (ten 9s and ten 5s).

Each student also needs two copies of *Digit Cards 0–9* (two each of the digits 0–9). Either cut out the cards using a paper cutter before class or have students cut out the cards. If you use *Digit Cards 0–9*, students will be multiplying 9s and 5s by the digits 0–9.

A deck of playing cards per pair can be substituted for the *Digit Cards 0–9*. Remove the face cards from each deck of playing cards before distributing them to the students. The aces can stand for 1s. If you use playing cards, students will be multiplying 9s and 5s by the numbers 1–10.

Teaching the Game

This card game provides practice with multiplication combinations with 5 and 9. It makes a good homework assignment after you introduce it in class.

Before playing the game, discuss strategies for multiplication with 5 or 9. Skip counting is useful for 5s, but your students may have others. Multiplication by 9 results in many patterns that can be helpful. Remind students of the patterns they found in the following:

$$1 \times 9 = 9$$
$$2 \times 9 = 18$$
$$3 \times 9 = 27$$
$$4 \times 9 = 36$$
$$5 \times 9 = 45$$
$$6 \times 9 = 54$$
$$7 \times 9 = 63$$
$$8 \times 9 = 72$$
$$9 \times 9 = 81$$
$$10 \times 9 = 90$$

Some patterns are merely interesting, but some can be practical. Two particularly useful patterns are that the sum of the digits is always 9 (e.g., $7 \times 9 = 63$; $6 + 3 = 9$) and that the first digit of the product is always one less than the other factor (e.g., $3 \times 9 = \mathbf{2}7$; The "2" is one less than the "3"). (See DPP item C.)

Find and describe a pattern you can use to help you multiply by 9.

After discussing strategies for the 5s and 9s, discuss the directions for the game by reading the *9 to 5 War* Game Pages in the *Student Guide*. Model the game with a student volunteer after distributing materials and discussing the directions. A sample game setup is shown in the *Student Guide*.

Math Facts

The *9 to 5 War* Game provides practice with the multiplication facts for the fives and nines.

Homework and Practice

Students play this game at home using a deck of playing cards. They need to take home their *9 to 5 War Cards* from the *Discovery Assignment Book* as well as their *Student Guide* Game Pages that have the directions for the game.

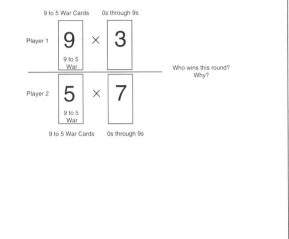

Rules

1. Players place their two piles face down in front of them.

2. Each player turns over two cards, one from the 9s and 5s pile, and one from the other pile.

3. Each player should say a number sentence that tells the product of his or her two cards. Whoever has the greater product wins all four cards.

4. If there is a tie, then each player turns over two more cards. The player with the greater product of the second pairs wins all eight cards.

5. Play for ten minutes or until the players run out of cards. The player with more cards at the end is the winner.

Student Guide - page 176

Variations

1. Whoever has the *smaller* product takes the cards.

2. Play with more than two players.

3. Each player is given only one pile of cards (playing cards with face cards removed or *Digit Cards*). Each player takes the top two cards from his or her pile and multiplies the numbers. The player with the larger product wins all four cards. This game practices all the facts—it does not just focus on the 9s and 5s.

Student Guide - page 177

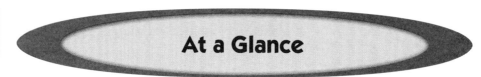

Math Facts and Daily Practice and Problems

The *9 to 5 War* Game provides practice with multiplication facts for the fives and nines.

Teaching the Game

1. Discuss strategies for multiplication with 5 or 9.
2. Discuss the directions for the game by reading the *9 to 5 War* Game Pages in the *Student Guide.*
3. Students prepare a stack of *9 to 5 War Cards* and a stack of cards with other digits.
4. Model the game.
5. Students play the game.

Homework

Ask students to play the game at home.

Notes:

Small Multiplication Tables

×	0	1	2	3	4	5	6	7	8	9	10
0	0	0	0	0	0	0	0	0	0	0	0
1	0	1	2	3	4	5	6	7	8	9	10
2	0	2	4	6	8	10	12	14	16	18	20
3	0	3	6	9	12	15	18	21	24	27	30
4	0	4	8	12	16	20	24	28	32	36	40
5	0	5	10	15	20	25	30	35	40	45	50
6	0	6	12	18	24	30	36	42	48	54	60
7	0	7	14	21	28	35	42	49	56	63	70
8	0	8	16	24	32	40	48	56	64	72	80
9	0	9	18	27	36	45	54	63	72	81	90
10	0	10	20	30	40	50	60	70	80	90	100

×	0	1	2	3	4	5	6	7	8	9	10
0	0	0	0	0	0	0	0	0	0	0	0
1	0	1	2	3	4	5	6	7	8	9	10
2	0	2	4	6	8	10	12	14	16	18	20
3	0	3	6	9	12	15	18	21	24	27	30
4	0	4	8	12	16	20	24	28	32	36	40
5	0	5	10	15	20	25	30	35	40	45	50
6	0	6	12	18	24	30	36	42	48	54	60
7	0	7	14	21	28	35	42	49	56	63	70
8	0	8	16	24	32	40	48	56	64	72	80
9	0	9	18	27	36	45	54	63	72	81	90
10	0	10	20	30	40	50	60	70	80	90	100

×	0	1	2	3	4	5	6	7	8	9	10
0	0	0	0	0	0	0	0	0	0	0	0
1	0	1	2	3	4	5	6	7	8	9	10
2	0	2	4	6	8	10	12	14	16	18	20
3	0	3	6	9	12	15	18	21	24	27	30
4	0	4	8	12	16	20	24	28	32	36	40
5	0	5	10	15	20	25	30	35	40	45	50
6	0	6	12	18	24	30	36	42	48	54	60
7	0	7	14	21	28	35	42	49	56	63	70
8	0	8	16	24	32	40	48	56	64	72	80
9	0	9	18	27	36	45	54	63	72	81	90
10	0	10	20	30	40	50	60	70	80	90	100

×	0	1	2	3	4	5	6	7	8	9	10
0	0	0	0	0	0	0	0	0	0	0	0
1	0	1	2	3	4	5	6	7	8	9	10
2	0	2	4	6	8	10	12	14	16	18	20
3	0	3	6	9	12	15	18	21	24	27	30
4	0	4	8	12	16	20	24	28	32	36	40
5	0	5	10	15	20	25	30	35	40	45	50
6	0	6	12	18	24	30	36	42	48	54	60
7	0	7	14	21	28	35	42	49	56	63	70
8	0	8	16	24	32	40	48	56	64	72	80
9	0	9	18	27	36	45	54	63	72	81	90
10	0	10	20	30	40	50	60	70	80	90	100

Discovery Assignment Book (p. 67)

Part 2. Mixed-Up Multiplication Tables

1.

×	2	3	5	9	10
4	8	12	20	36	40
6	12	18	30	54	60
7	14	21	35	63	70
8	16	24	40	72	80

Answers will vary.

2. **A.** 2   **B.** 8

C. 4   **D.** 10

E. 7   **F.** 8

G. 9   **H.** 6

Discovery Assignment Book - page 67

Discovery Assignment Book (p. 68)

Part 3. Addition and Subtraction Practice

A. 13,259

B. 14,446

C. 6646

D. 3074

E. 10,903

F. 2822: $10,500 - 7,500 = 3000.$

Part 4. Using Estimation

1. Mexico: 171,748; China: 41,861; Philippines: 40, 587; India: 39,072; Vietnam: 25,340.

2. Answers will vary. One possible solution is: 130,000; $170,000 - 40,000 = 130,000$ people.

3. Answers will vary. One possible solution is: 190,000; $20,000 + 170,000 = 190,000$ people.

4. Canada

5. Answers will vary. One possible solution is: 300,000. $40,000 - 10,000 = 30,000$ people.

6. Answers will vary based on estimates. One possible solution is $20,000 + 40,000 + 20,000 + 20,000 + 40,000 + 170,000 + 40,000 + 10,000 + 10,000 + 30,000 = 400,000$ immigrants.

Discovery Assignment Book - page 68

Left page content (Discovery Assignment Book - page 67):

Name _____ Date _____

Unit 6 Home Practice

PART 1 *Triangle Flash Cards: 9s*
Study for the quiz on the multiplication facts for the nines. Take home your *Triangle Flash Cards: 9s* and your list of facts you need to study.

Here's how to use the flash cards. Ask a family member to choose one flash card at a time. He or she should cover the corner containing the highest number. This number will be the answer to a multiplication fact. Multiply the two uncovered numbers.

Your teacher will tell you when the quiz on the 9s will be.

PART 2 Mixed-Up Multiplication Tables

1. Complete the table. Then, describe any patterns you see.

×	2	3	5	9	10
4					
6		18			
7					
8					

2. The letter *n* stands for a missing number. Find the missing number in each number sentence.
   A. $n \times 7 = 14$ **B.** $3 \times n = 24$ **C.** $n \times 4 = 16$ **D.** $n \times 8 = 80$
   E. $9 \times n = 63$ **F.** $n \times 8 = 64$ **G.** $4 \times n = 36$ **H.** $n \times 5 = 30$

PLACE VALUE PATTERNS   DAB • Grade 4 • Unit 6   **67**

Left page content (Discovery Assignment Book - page 68):

Name _____ Date _____

PART 3 Addition and Subtraction Practice
Use paper and pencil to solve the following problems. Use estimation to decide if your answers make sense. Explain your estimation strategy for F.

A. 4506 + 8753   **B.** 5388 + 9078   **C.** 9054 − 2408

D. 7617 − 4543   **E.** 3940 + 6963   **F.** 10,415 − 7593

PART 4 Using Estimation
The following table lists the number of people who immigrated to the United States from various countries in 2000. Use the information in the table to estimate the answers to the questions below. Use a separate sheet of paper to show what convenient numbers you chose to work with.

Country	Number of Immigrants	Country	Number of Immigrants
Canada	21,475	Mexico	171,748
China	41,861	Philippines	40,587
Dominican Republic	17,441	Romania	6,521
El Salvador	22,332	United Kingdom	14,532
India	39,072	Vietnam	25,340

1. Most immigrants came from which five countries listed in the table? List the countries and their number of immigrants. List the number of immigrants in order from largest to smallest.

2. About how many more people immigrated from Mexico than from China?

3. About how many people immigrated from Canada and Mexico combined?

4. The number of immigrants from El Salvador is about the same as the number of immigrants from which other country?

5. About how many more people came from India than Romania?

6. In 2000, the number of immigrants from all countries totaled about 850,000 people. About how many immigrants are reported in the table above? (*Hint:* Use a calculator to help you with your estimation.)

68   DAB • Grade 4 • Unit 6   PLACE VALUE PATTERNS

Discovery Assignment Book (p. 69)

Part 5. Numbers in the News

Millions			Thousands			Ones		
					9	8	3	5
				3	9	9	0	5
				4	2	3	1	9
			7	9	3	0	2	7
		4	1	3	0	2	4	3
		4	6	1	3	3	7	8
		7	9	3	1	4	3	5

nine thousand, eight hundred thirty-five

seven million, nine hundred thirty-one thousand, four hundred thirty-five

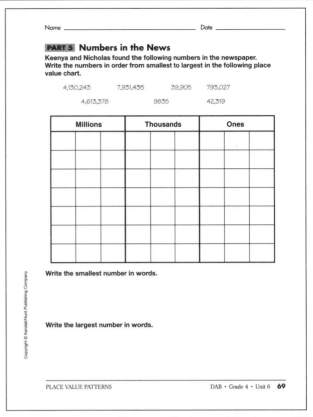

Discovery Assignment Book - page 69

Discovery Assignment Book (p. 70)

Part 6. Subtraction Count Backs

A. 9   B. 29
C. 90   D. 290
E. 24   F. 4
G. 2400 H. 40
I. 9   J. 49
K. 90   L. 4900

Descriptions of patterns will vary.

Part 7. Convenient Numbers

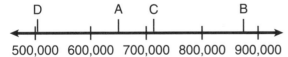

A. 650,000; 700,000
B. 870,000; 900,000
C. 720,000; 700,000
D. 510,000; 500,000

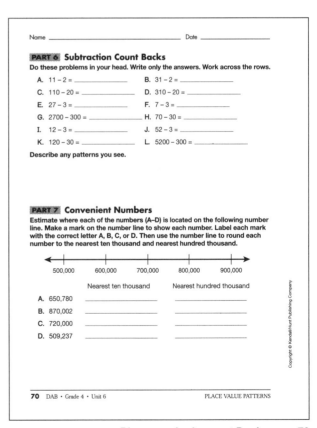

Discovery Assignment Book - page 70

Glossary

This glossary provides definitions of key vocabulary terms in the Grade 4 lessons. Locations of key vocabulary terms in the curriculum are included with each definition. Components Key: URG = *Unit Resource Guide* and SG = *Student Guide.*

A

Acre (URG Unit 6; SG Unit 6)
A measure of land area equal to 43,560 square feet.

Acute Angle (URG Unit 2 & Unit 9; SG Unit 2)
An angle that measures less than 90°.

All-Partials Algorithm
(URG Unit 7; SG Unit 7)
A paper-and-pencil method for solving multiplication problems. Each partial product is recorded on a separate line. (*See also* partial product.)

$$\begin{array}{r} 186 \\ \times\ 3 \\ \hline 18 \\ 240 \\ 300 \\ \hline 558 \end{array}$$

Angle (URG Unit 2; SG Unit 2)
The amount of turning or the amount of opening between two rays that have the same endpoint.

Angle of Turning (URG Unit 9)
The smallest angle through which a figure can be turned about the center of turning so that the figure coincides with itself.

Area (SG Unit 2)
The area of a shape is the amount of space it covers, measured in square units.

Array (URG Unit 4)
An array is an arrangement of elements into a rectangular pattern of (horizontal) rows and (vertical) columns.

Average (URG Unit 1 & Unit 5; SG Unit 1 & Unit 5)
A number that can be used to represent a typical value in a set of data. (*See also* mean and median.)

B

Base (of an exponent) (SG Unit 4)
When exponents are used, the number being multiplied. In $3^4 = 3 \times 3 \times 3 \times 3 = 81$, the 3 is the base and the 4 is the exponent. The 3 is multiplied by itself 4 times.

Base-Ten Board (URG Unit 3; SG Unit 3)
A tool to help children organize base-ten pieces when they are representing numbers.

Base-Ten Pieces (URG Unit 3; SG Unit 3)
A set of manipulatives used to model our number system as shown in the figure below. Note that a skinny is made of 10 bits, a flat is made of 100 bits, and a pack is made of 1000 bits.

Nickname	Picture	Shorthand
bit	⬜	•
skinny	▭	/
flat	▱	⬭
pack	▦	⬭

Base-Ten Shorthand (URG Unit 3; SG Unit 3)
A pictorial representation of the base-ten pieces is shown in Unit 3.

Benchmarks (URG Unit 6; SG Unit 6)
Numbers convenient for comparing and ordering numbers, e.g., $0, \frac{1}{2}, 1$ are convenient benchmarks for comparing and ordering fractions.

Best-Fit Line (URG Unit 5; SG Unit 5)
The line that comes closest to the points on a point graph.

Binning Data (URG Unit 13)
Placing data from a data set with a large number of values or large range into intervals in order to more easily see patterns in the data.

Bit (URG Unit 3 & Unit 6; SG Unit 3)
A cube that measures 1 cm on each edge. It is the smallest of the base-ten pieces and is often used to represent 1. (*See also* base-ten pieces.)

C

Categorical Variable (URG Unit 1; SG Unit 1)
Variables with values that are not numbers. (*See also* variable and value.)

Center of Turning (URG Unit 9; SG Unit 9)
A point on a plane figure around which it is turned. In particular, the point about which an object with turn symmetry is rotated.

Centimeter (SG Unit 10)
A unit of length in the metric system. A centimeter is $\frac{1}{100}$ of a meter.

Certain Event (URG Unit 14; SG Unit 14)
An event that has a probability of 1 (100%).

Common Fraction (URG Unit 10)
Any fraction that is written with a numerator and denominator that are whole numbers. For example, $\frac{3}{4}$ and $\frac{9}{4}$ are both common fractions. (*See also* decimal fraction.)

Commutative Property of Multiplication
(URG Unit 3 & Unit 4)
This is also known as the Order Property of Multiplication. Changing the order of the factors does not change the product. For example, $3 \times 5 = 5 \times 3 = 15$. Using variables, $n \times m = m \times n$.

Composite Number (URG Unit 4)
A number that has more than two distinct factors. For example, 9 has three factors (1, 3, 9) so it is a composite number.

Convenient Number (URG Unit 1 & Unit 7; SG Unit 7)
A number used in computation that is close enough to give a good estimate, but is also easy to compute with mentally, e.g., 25 and 30 are convenient numbers for 27.

Cubic Centimeter (URG Unit 8; SG Unit 8)
The volume of a cube that is one centimeter long on each edge.

D

Decimal (URG Unit 3)
1. A number written using the base-ten place value system.
2. A number containing a decimal point. (*See also* decimal fraction.)

Decimal Fraction (URG Unit 10)
A fraction written as a decimal. For example, 0.75 and 0.4 are decimal fractions and $\frac{75}{100}$ and $\frac{4}{10}$ are called common fractions.

Decimeter (URG Unit 10; SG Unit 10)
A unit of length in the metric system. A decimeter is $\frac{1}{10}$ of a meter.

Degree (URG Unit 2; SG Unit 2)
A degree (°) is a unit of measure for angles. There are 360 degrees in a circle.

Denominator (URG Unit 10 & Unit 12; SG Unit 10 & Unit 12)
The number below the line in a fraction. The denominator indicates the number of equal parts in which the unit whole is divided. For example, the 5 is the denominator in the fraction $\frac{2}{5}$. In this case the unit whole is divided into five equal parts.

Dividend (URG Unit 3; SG Unit 3)
The number that is divided in a division problem, e.g., 12 is the dividend in $12 \div 3 = 4$.

Divisible (URG Unit 7; SG Unit 7)
A number a is divisible by a number b, if there is no remainder when a is divided by b. For example, 12 is divisible by 4 ($12 \div 4 = 3$), but **not** by 5 ($12 \div 5 = 2$ R2).

Division Sentence (SG Unit 3)
A number sentence involving division.

Divisor (URG Unit 3 & Unit 8; SG Unit 3 & Unit 8)
In a division problem, the number by which another number is divided. In the problem $12 \div 4 = 3$, the 4 is the divisor, the 12 is the dividend, and the 3 is the quotient.

E

Edge (URG Unit 9; SG Unit 9)
A line segment where two faces of a three-dimensional figure meet.

Equilateral Triangle (URG Unit 2 & Unit 9; SG Unit 9)
A triangle with all sides and all angles equal.

Equivalent Fractions (URG Unit 12; SG Unit 12)
Fractions that have the same value, e.g., $\frac{2}{4} = \frac{1}{2}$.

Estimate (URG Unit 3, Unit 6, & Unit 7; SG Unit 7)
1. (verb) To find *about* how many.
2. (noun) An approximate number.

Even Number (SG Unit 4)
Numbers that are multiples of 2 (2, 4, 6, 8, etc.) are called even numbers.

Exponent (URG Unit 4; SG Unit 4)
The number of times the base is multiplied by itself. In $3^4 = 3 \times 3 \times 3 \times 3 = 81$, the 3 is the base and the 4 is the exponent. The 3 is multiplied by itself 4 times.

Extrapolation (URG Unit 5; SG Unit 5)
Using patterns in data to make predictions or to estimate values that lie beyond the range of values in the set of data.

F

Face (URG Unit 9; SG Unit 9)
A plane figure that is one side of a three-dimensional figure.

Fact Family (URG Unit 3 & Unit 8; SG Unit 3 & Unit 8)
Related math facts, e.g., $3 \times 4 = 12$, $4 \times 3 = 12$, $12 \div 3 = 4$, $12 \div 4 = 3$.

Factor (URG Unit 3 & Unit 4; SG Unit 3, Unit 4, & Unit 7)
1. In a multiplication problem, the numbers that are multiplied together. In the problem $3 \times 4 = 12$, 3 and 4 are the factors.
2. Whole numbers that can be multiplied together to get a number. That is, numbers that divide a number evenly, e.g., 1, 2, 3, 4, 6, and 12 are all the factors of 12.

Factor Tree (URG Unit 4; SG Unit 4)
A diagram that shows the prime factorization of a number.

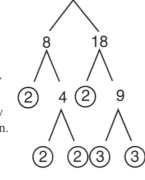

Fair Game or Fair Number Cube (URG Unit 14)
A game in which it is equally likely that any player will win. A number cube is fair if all the faces are equally likely to appear.

Fewest Pieces Rule (URG Unit 3 & Unit 10; SG Unit 3)
Using the least number of base-ten pieces to represent a number. (*See also* base-ten pieces.)

Fixed Variables (URG Unit 1, Unit 2, & Unit 5; SG Unit 5)
Variables in an experiment that are held constant or not changed.

Flat (URG Unit 3 & Unit 6; SG Unit 3)
A block that measures 1 cm $\times$ 10 cm $\times$ 10 cm. It is one of the base-ten pieces and is often used to represent 100. (*See also* base-ten pieces.)

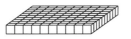

Forgiving Method of Division (URG Unit 13; SG Unit 13)
A paper-and-pencil method for division in which successive partial quotients are chosen and partial products are subtracted from the dividend, until the remainder is less than the divisor. The sum of the partial quotients is the quotient. For example, $644 \div 7$ can be solved as shown at the right. This method of division is called the forgiving method because it "forgives" estimates of the partial quotients that are too low.

$$
\begin{array}{r}
92 \\
7\,\overline{\smash{)}\,644} \\
\end{array}
\quad
\begin{array}{r|r}
644 & \\
140 & 20 \\
\hline
504 & \\
350 & 50 \\
\hline
154 & \\
140 & 20 \\
\hline
14 & \\
14 & 2 \\
\hline
0 & 92 \\
\end{array}
$$

Front-End Estimation (URG Unit 3)
Estimation by looking at the left-most digit.

Function (URG Unit 15)
A rule that assigns to any input number exactly one output number. More generally, a rule that assigns to the elements of one set (the domain) exactly one element of another set (the target).

G

H

Hexagon (URG Unit 2)
A six-sided polygon.

Hieroglyphics (URG Unit 11)
An ancient Egyptian form of writing.

I

Identity Property of Multiplication (URG Unit 3)
This is also known as the Property of One for Multiplication. One times any number is that number. Using variables, $n \times 1 = n$.

Impossible Event (URG Unit 14; SG Unit 14)
An event that has a probability of 0 or 0%.

Infinite (URG Unit 9)
Cannot be counted in a finite amount of time. More than any number.

Interpolation (URG Unit 5; SG Unit 5)
Making predictions or estimating values that lie between data points in a set of data.

Intersect (SG Unit 9)
To meet or cross.

J

K

L

Likely Event (URG Unit 14; SG Unit 14)
An event that has a high probability of occurring.

Line (URG Unit 9; SG Unit 9)
A set of points that form a straight path extending infinitely in two directions.

Line Segment (URG Unit 9; SG Unit 9)
A part of a line between and including two points called the endpoints.

Line of Symmetry (URG Unit 9; SG Unit 9)
A line is a line of symmetry for a plane figure if, when the figure is folded along this line, the two parts match exactly.

Line Symmetry (URG Unit 9; SG Unit 9)
A figure has line symmetry if it has at least one line of symmetry.

Liter (SG Unit 8)
Metric unit used to measure volume. A liter is a little more than a quart.

M

Manipulated Variable (URG Unit 5 & Unit 10; SG Unit 5)
In an experiment, the variable with values known at the beginning of the experiment. The experimenter often chooses these values before data is collected. The manipulated variable is often called the independent variable.

Mass (URG Unit 8 & Unit 15; SG Unit 15)
The amount of matter in an object.

Mean (URG Unit 1 & Unit 5; SG Unit 5)
An average of a set of numbers that is found by adding the values of the data and dividing by the number of values.

Measurement Division (URG Unit 4)
Division as equal grouping. The total number of objects and the number of objects in each group are known. The number of groups is the unknown. For example, tulip bulbs come in packages of 8. If 216 bulbs are sold, how many packages are sold?

Measurement Error
The unavoidable error that occurs due to the limitations inherent to any measurement instrument.

Median (URG Unit 1 & Unit 5; SG Unit 1 & Unit 5)
For a set with an odd number of data arranged in order, it is the middle number. For an even number of data arranged in order, it is the number halfway between the two middle numbers.

Megabit (URG Unit 6)
A base-ten model that is a cube with an edge of length 100 cm. It represents 1,000,000 since it has a volume of 1,000,000 cubic cm.

Meniscus (URG Unit 8; SG Unit 8)
The curved surface formed when a liquid creeps up the side of a container (for example, a graduated cylinder).

Meter (SG Unit 10)
A unit of length in the metric system. A meter is a bit more that 39 inches.

Milliliter (ml) (URG Unit 8; SG Unit 8)
A measure of capacity in the metric system that is the volume of a cube that is one centimeter long on each side.

Millimeter (SG Unit 10)
A unit of length in the metric system. A millimeter is one-thousandth of a meter, i.e., one-tenth of a centimeter.

Millions Period (URG Unit 6; SG Unit 6)
The sequence of digits (if any) in the millions place, the ten-millions place, and the hundred millions place. In the number 12,**456,**789,987 the millions period is in bold type.

Multiple (URG Unit 4 & Unit 7; SG Unit 4 & Unit 7)
A number is a multiple of another number if it is evenly divisible by that number. For example, 12 is a multiple of 2 since 2 divides 12 evenly.

Multiplicand (URG Unit 11)
Either of the numbers being multiplied in a multiplication problem.

N

Negative Number (URG Unit 3; SG Unit 3)
A number less than zero; a number to the left of zero on a horizontal number line.

Net (URG Unit 9; SG Unit 9)
A way of representing the surface of a three-dimensional solid in two-dimensions. A net can be obtained by cutting the surface along edges until it can be laid flat on a plane.

Number Sentence
An equation or inequality with numbers. For example, $3 \times 2 + 5 = 10 + 1$ and $2 < 3 + 1$

Numeral (URG Unit 3)
A symbol used to represent a number.

Numerator (URG Unit 10 & Unit 12; SG Unit 10 & Unit 12)
The number written above the line in a fraction. For example, the 2 is the numerator in the fraction $\frac{2}{5}$. (*See also* denominator.)

Numerical Variable (URG Unit 1; SG Unit 1)
Variables with values that are numbers. (*See also* variable and value.)

O

Obtuse Angle (URG Unit 2 & Unit 9; SG Unit 2)
An angle that measures more than 90°.

Odd Number (SG Unit 4)
Numbers that are not multiples of 2 (1, 3, 5 ,7, etc.) are called odd numbers.

Ones Period (URG Unit 6; SG Unit 6)
The sequence of digits (if any) in the ones place, the tens place, and the hundreds place. In the number 12,456,789,**987** the ones period is in bold type.

Operation (SG Unit 7)
A process that takes two numbers and results in a third. This, more precisely, is called a binary operation. For example, addition, subtraction, multiplication, and division are operations.

Order of Operations (URG Unit 7; SG Unit 7)
A convention that determines how to find the value of an expression that has more than one operation.

P

Pack (URG Unit 3; SG Unit 3)
A cube that measures 10 cm on each edge. It is one of the base-ten pieces and is often used to represent 1000. (*See also* base-ten pieces.)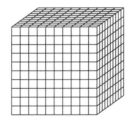

Papyrus (URG Unit 11)
A type of writing paper used by the ancient Egyptians.

Parallel Lines (URG Unit 9; SG Unit 9)
Lines that are in the same direction. In the plane, parallel lines are lines that do not intersect.

Parallelogram (URG Unit 9; SG Unit 9)
A quadrilateral with two pairs of parallel sides.

Partitive Division (URG Unit 4 & Unit 13)
Division as equal sharing. The total number of objects and the number of groups are known. The number of objects in each group is the unknown. For example, Frank has 144 marbles that he divides equally into 6 groups. How many marbles are in each group?

Perimeter (URG Unit 2; SG Unit 2)
The distance around a two-dimensional shape.

Period (URG Unit 6; SG Unit 6)
A group of three places in a large number, starting on the right, often separated by commas as shown at the right.

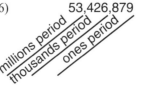
53,426,879
millions period
thousands period
ones period

Perpendicular (URG Unit 9; SG Unit 9)
Perpendicular lines are lines that meet at right angles.

Perspective (URG Unit 9)
The art of drawing solid objects on a flat surface so that it produces the same impression as do the actual objects when viewed from a particular point.

Point (URG Unit 9)
An exact position in the plane or in space.

Polygon (URG Unit 9; SG Unit 9)
A two-dimensional connected figure made of line segments in which each endpoint of every side meets with an endpoint of exactly one other side.

Polyhedron (URG Unit 9)
A connected geometric solid whose surface is made of polygons.

Portfolio (URG Unit 2)
A collection of student work that shows how a student's skills, attitudes, and knowledge change over time.

Positive Number (URG Unit 3; SG Unit 3)
A number greater than zero; a number to the right of zero on a horizontal number line.

Powers of Two (URG Unit 6; SG Unit 6)
2 multiplied by itself a certain number of times. $2^1 = 2$, $2^2 = 2 \times 2 = 4$, $2^3 = 2 \times 2 \times 2 = 8$, etc.

Prime Factor (URG Unit 4; SG Unit 4)
A factor of a number that is itself prime.

Prime Number (URG Unit 4; SG Unit 4)
A number that has exactly two factors, itself and 1. For example, 7 has exactly two distinct factors, 1 and 7.

Prism (URG Unit 9; SG Unit 9)
A polyhedron that has two congruent faces, called bases, that are parallel to each other, and all other faces are parallelograms. If the other faces are rectangles the prism is called a right prism.

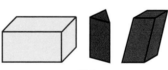

Prisms   Not a prism

Probability (URG Unit 14; SG Unit 14)
A number from 0 to 1 (0% to 100%) that describes how likely an event is to happen. The closer that the probability of an event is to one, the more likely the event will happen.

Product (URG Unit 3; SG Unit 3 & Unit 4)
The answer to a multiplication problem. In the problem $3 \times 4 = 12$, 12 is the product.

Q

Quadrilateral (URG Unit 9; SG Unit 2 & Unit 9)
A polygon with four sides. (*See also* polygon.)

Quick Paper-and-Pencil Method for Addition
(URG Unit 3; SG Unit 3)
A traditional method for
adding multidigit numbers.
See example at right:

$$\begin{array}{r} \overset{1}{1}\overset{1}{3}26 \\ +575 \\ \hline 1901 \end{array}$$

Quick Paper-and-Pencil Method for Subtraction (SG Unit 3)
A traditional method for subtraction.
For example:

$$\begin{array}{r} 1237 \\ -459 \\ \hline 778 \end{array}$$

Quotient (URG Unit 3 & Unit 13; SG Unit 3 & Unit 8)
The answer to a division problem. In the problem
$12 \div 3 = 4$, the 4 is the quotient.

R

Ray (URG Unit 9; SG Unit 9)
A part of a line that has one endpoint and extends
indefinitely in one direction.

Recording Sheet (URG Unit 3; SG Unit 3)
A place value chart used for addition and subtraction
problems.

Rectangle (URG Unit 2 & Unit 9)
A quadrilateral with four right angles.

Reflex Angle (URG Unit 2)
An angle larger than 180° but less than 360°.

Regular (URG Unit 9)
A polygon is regular if all sides are of equal length and
all angles are equal.

Remainder (URG Unit 13)
Something that remains or is left after a whole number
division problem. The portion of the dividend that is not
evenly divisible by the divisor, e.g., $16 \div 5 = 3$ with
1 as a remainder.

Responding Variable (URG Unit 5 & Unit 10;
SG Unit 5)
The variable whose values result from the experiment.
Experimenters find the values of the responding variable
by doing the experiment. The responding variable is often
called the dependent variable.

Rhombus (URG Unit 2)
A quadrilateral with four sides of equal length.

Right Angle (URG Unit 2 & Unit 9; SG Unit 2)
An angle that measures 90°.

Roman Numeral (URG Unit 3; SG Unit 3)
A system of representing numbers used by the
Romans. The symbol I represents 1, V represents
five, X represents ten, etc.

Rounded Number (URG Unit 6 & Unit 7)
See rounding.

Rounding (URG Unit 6)
Replacing a number with the nearest convenient number.
Numbers are often rounded to the nearest whole number,
ten, hundred, fifty, etc.

S

Skinny (URG Unit 3 & Unit 6; SG Unit 3)
A block that measures 1 cm × 1 cm
× 10 cm. It is one of the base-ten
pieces that is often used to represent 10.
(*See also* base-ten pieces.)

Solid (URG Unit 9; SG Unit 9)
A three-dimensional figure that has volume greater
than 0.

Square (URG Unit 2)
A polygon with four equal sides and four right angles.

Square Inch (SG Unit 2)
The area of a square with a side length of one inch.

Square Number (URG Unit 4; SG Unit 4)
A number that is the result of multiplying a whole
number by itself. For example, 36 is a square number
since $36 = 6 \times 6$.

Square Root (URG Unit 15)
The square root of a number N is the number whose square
is N. The symbol for square root is $\sqrt{}$. For example,
the square root of 25 is 5, since $5 \times 5 = 25$. In symbols
we write $\sqrt{25} = 5$. The square root of 26 is not a whole
number.

Subtractive Principle (URG Unit 3; SG Unit 3)
A method of interpreting certain Roman numerals.
For example, IX represents 9 while XI represents 11.

Super Bit (URG Unit 6)
A base-ten model that is a cube with an edge of length
10 cm. It represents 1,000 since it has a volume of 1,000
cubic centimeters. It is usually called a pack.

Super Flat (URG Unit 6)
A base-ten model that is a rectangular solid that measures
10 cm × 100 cm × 100 cm. It represents 100,000 since
it has a volume of 100,000 cubic cm.

Super Skinny (URG Unit 6)
A base-ten model that is a rectangular solid that measures
10 cm × 10 cm × 100 cm. It represents 10,000 since it
has a volume of 10,000 cubic cm.

Survey (SG Unit 13)
An investigation conducted by collecting data from a sample of a population and then analyzing it. Usually surveys are used to make predictions about the entire population.

T

Tally
A way of recording a count by making marks. Usually tallies are grouped in fives. ꟷꟷꟷ |||

Ten Percent (10%) (URG Unit 6 & Unit 7)
10 out of every hundred or $\frac{1}{10}$.

Thousands Period (URG Unit 6; SG Unit 6)
The sequence of digits (if any) in the thousands place, the ten-thousands place, and the hundred-thousands place. In the number 12,456,**789**,987 the thousands period is in bold type.

TIMS Laboratory Method (URG Unit 1; SG Unit 1)
A method that students use to organize experiments and investigations. It involves four phases: draw, collect, graph, and explore. It is a way to help students learn about the scientific method.

Translational Symmetry (URG Unit 9)
A pattern has translational symmetry if there is a translation that moves the pattern so it coincides with itself.

Trapezoid (URG Unit 2)
A quadrilateral with exactly one pair of parallel sides.

Triangle (URG Unit 2)
A polygon with three sides.

Turn-Around Facts (URG Unit 3; SG Unit 3)
Multiplication facts that have the same factors but in a different order, e.g., $3 \times 4 = 12$ and $4 \times 3 = 12$. (*See also* commutative property of multiplication.)

Turn-Around Rule (URG Unit 4)
A term used to describe the commutative property of multiplication. (*See also* commutative property of multiplication.)

Turn Symmetry (URG Unit 9; SG Unit 9)
A figure has turn symmetry if it can be rotated around a point (called the center of turning) through an angle less than 360° and so that the turned figure matches the original.

Type of Turn Symmetry (URG Unit 9)
The number of times a figure coincides with itself when it is rotated about its center of turning. For example, a square has 4-fold turn symmetry. This is also called $\frac{1}{4}$ turn symmetry.

U

Undefined (Division by Zero) (URG Unit 13; SG Unit 13)
We say division by 0 is undefined because there is no number that satisfies the definition of division when 0 is the divisor. For example, if there were a number $N = 3 \div 0$, it would be the unique number N that makes $N \times 0 = 3$ a true statement. There is no such N.

Unlikely Event (URG Unit 14; SG Unit 14)
An event that has small probability.

V

Value (URG Unit 1; SG Unit 1)
The possible outcomes of a variable. For example, red, green, and blue are possible values for the variable *color*. Two meters and 1.65 meters are possible values for the variable *length.*

Variable (URG Unit 1; SG Unit 1)
1. An attribute or quantity that changes or varies. (*See also* categorical variable and numerical variable.)
2. A symbol that can stand for a variable.

Vertex (URG Unit 2 & Unit 9; SG Unit 2 & Unit 9)
The common endpoint of two rays or line segments.

Volume (URG Unit 8 & Unit 9; SG Unit 8)
The measure of the amount of space occupied by an object.

Volume by Displacement (SG Unit 8)
A way of measuring volume by measuring the amount of water (or some other fluid) it displaces.

W

Weight (URG Unit 15; SG Unit 15)
A measure of the pull of gravity on an object. One unit for measuring weight is the pound.

X

Y

Z

Zero Property of Multiplication (URG Unit 3)
Any number times zero is zero. Using variables, $n \times 0 = 0$.